THE
RIGHT-
BRAIN
EXPERIENCE

MARILEE ZDENEK

THE RIGHT-BRAIN EXPERIENCE

An Intimate Program to Free the Powers of Your Imagination

McGraw-Hill Book Company

New York St. Louis San Francisco
Auckland Bogotá Guatemala
Hamburg Johannesburg Lisbon London Madrid
Mexico Montreal New Delhi Panama Paris San Juan
São Paulo Singapore Sydney Tokyo Toronto

First paperback edition, 1985.

1 2 3 4 5 6 7 8 9 SEM SEM 8 7 6 5

ISBN 0-07-072744-9

LIBRARY OF CONGRESS CATALOGING IN PUBLICATION DATA

Zdenek, Marilee.
The right brain experience.
Bibliography: p.
Includes index.
1. Creative thinking.   2. Problem solving. I. Title.
BF411.A34   1983   153.3'5   83-9842
ISBN 0-07-072737-6 (H.C.)
      0-07-072744-9 (pbk.)

Book design by Virginia M. Soulé

All mandalas designed by Hal Fletcher, Jr.

*The exercises in this book should not be performed by
anyone whom a physician has diagnosed as emotionally disturbed.*

for Al
who makes all the difference

Contents

Part III
YOUR PERSONAL PROGRAM 123

Each of the above chapters has eleven exercise sections, described below, to be followed by program-users. For maximum benefit the exercises should be done in chronological order.

Category 1   Outsmarting the Left Brain

Category 2   Biofeedback Training

Category 3   Guided Visualization

Category 4   Transitional Objects

Category 5   Other-Hand Writing

Category 6   Sensory Stimulation

Category 7   Fantasy

Category 8   Dream Work

Category 9   Free Association

Category 10 Gifts from the Right Brain

Category 11 Affirmations

Introduction

Creativity and its relationship to the right hemisphere of the brain is a subject of considerable interest, not only to scientists, but to all people who desire to learn more about how to stimulate the imagination effectively. As a psychiatrist/psychoanalyst who works in right-brain research, I am impressed by Marilee Zdenek's program for enhancing creativity, which is based on essential scientific data.

The neurophysiological findings of Roger Sperry, Joseph Bogen and Michael Gazzaniga revealed that each hemisphere of the brain processes information differently and has its own areas of specialization. These findings stimulated an abundance of experimental and clinical research.

Surgically splitting the connection between the two cerebral hemispheres made it possible to observe each side of the brain separately. It was demonstrated that the left hemisphere specializes in verbal, logical and linear thinking and cannot see the woods for the trees, so to speak, while the right hemisphere specializes in holistic, visual and spatial perceptions and senses the whole forest. In addition to the perception of the whole gestalt, the right hemisphere seems to represent feelings, speaking an "affective language."

In the 1970's, I had the privilege to be introduced to twelve split-brain people by Dr. Bogen and, for the last ten years, have performed psychiatric examinations on these patients and their relatives. I found that the split-brain people could very seldom recollect dreams or fantasies; when they did, these dreams and fantasies were unimaginative, rigid, utilitarian, and tied to reality. Bogen and I found that these split-brain people could not verbalize their feelings and were not able to express any imaginative thoughts.

These clinical observations support the findings of Bogen and Bogen that a blocked exchange between the two sides of the brain results in a lack of creativity. Especially the artist needs the openness toward the "other side of the brain," i.e., the right hemisphere.

Marilee Zdenek has transformed these scientific findings into a language full of intuition and poetry. In *The Right-Brain Experience*, she enriches our understanding of the individual potentialities we possess particularly in our right hemisphere.

Her interviews with people who have achieved outstanding success reveal a degree of empathic subtlety which is unfortunately too often brushed aside in our daily practice of psychiatry and psychotherapy, which should combine both science and art.

The six days of Marilee Zdenek's workshop of *The Right-Brain Experience* amalgamate ancient forms of meditation with modern techniques of relaxation and imagery. She draws from the insights of Freud, Jung, Winnecott, and some modern ego-psychologists such as Erik Erikson.

The author's intuition and enthusiasm lead the reader to encounter and to experience his or her own creative potentialities. In this process, we liberate ourselves from the over-critical voice of our conscience which is usually expressed in the logical-sequential style of the left hemisphere. By stimulating the right side of the brain, we awaken the powers of imagination which are frequently ignored.

Mrs. Zdenek's optimistic build-up of self-esteem seems to me a very helpful counter-weight to the daily confrontation with misery and depression in our world, which is particularly evident in the office of a psychoanalyst. Marilee Zdenek's book facilitates the reader's ability to experience life—as the poet Baudelaire expressed it—as a "forest of symbols," as a journey of infinite self-discovery and creative expression.

Klaus D. Hoppe, M.D., Ph.D.
Assoc. Professor of Clinical Psychiatry,
University of California at Los Angeles;
Director of Research and Continuing Medical Education,
The Hacker Clinic

Acknowledgements

The Right-Brain Experience had its genesis when the late Robert Kirsch encouraged me to explore the correlation between right brain stimulation and the creative process. Years later, Barbara Goldsmith, Frank Perry and Paula Nelson urged me to translate my research into a book. I am deeply grateful to each of them for their encouragement and support.

I appreciate the enthusiastic response of my agent, Don Congdon, who made an important suggestion that broadened the scope of this material. I wish to thank my editor, Lou Ashworth, for her expert advice, which has been most helpful.

The following medical doctors and scientific researchers have given generously of their time and expertise, reading the work in process and offering invaluable contributions during the development of this book. I am grateful for their assistance and encouragement. Klaus D. Hoppe, M.D., psychoanalyst, shared knowledge derived from his years of research on split-brain patients and provided significant medical papers and general suggestions that improved this book. Bruce W. Christianson, M.D., psychiatrist, enriched my understanding of imagery and its contribution to creativity and offered assistance through various difficult stages. Stanley J. Leiken, M.D., psychoanalyst, increased my awareness of the role of dreams and free association in deciphering important messages from the unconscious; his encouragement has been a strong sustaining factor. James S. Grotstein, M.D., psychoanalyst, affirmed the value of my use of imagery to enhance creativity and instilled confidence on the weariest of days. John R. F. Penido, M.D., thoracic surgeon, was a great provider of fascinating articles and good cheer. My step-son, Gene W. Zdenek, M.D., ophthalmic surgeon, offered helpful advice and perceptive comments. Jay Myers, who is currently involved in split-brain research at Cal Tech, was an invaluable source of information; his involvement through each stage of revisions has been of enormous benefit. My deepest appreciation is to my husband, Albert N. Zdenek, M.D., general practitioner, for his medical comments and constant encouragement—above all, for his nurturing spirit.

I am also indebted to those people who allowed me to interview them and to those students and clients involved in the testing of the right-brain exercises. Hal Fletcher, Jr., provided fine graphic designs in the mandalas and chart he created for this book. General assistance from Tamara Fletcher is greatly appreciated.

Amy Louise Shapiro was my first reader, and her insights and sensitivity have made a substantial contribution to the material. Comments from Perla Earle were always helpful. My daughter, Gina, worked through many long days and nights as my secretary, not only transferring each day's work onto the computer, but offering perceptive suggestions for which I am most grateful.

"What you can do, or dream you can, begin it;
Boldness has genius, power and magic in it."

—GOETHE

PART I

POWERS OF THE MIND

1

An Invitation

Years ago, a barefoot child in Rome sat on a high wall, watching a man below. "Ay, signore," he called, "why are you hitting that rock?" Michelangelo looked up and called back to the boy: "Because there's an angel inside and it wants to come out!"

What an extraordinary perception of the creative act. So often we think of creativity as the conscious, willful expression of our well-designed ideas. To Michelangelo, creating the statue required a far different attitude; he would chip away at the rock that imprisoned the angel until the final work of art was set free.

"The Right-Brain Experience" is designed to do for you and your creativity what that attitude did for Michelangelo and his angel. Your angel or mine may not be as exquisite as his; even so, there are tools we can use to chip away at the hardened approach toward the creative act. We can set the angel free. The choice is ours.

Most people yearn to be more creative. Many people feel that writers, painters, musicians, designers, and other artistic types have the corner on creativity. This is a limiting assumption. There is an artist in each of us. Powers of imagination and insight exist in the deepest regions of our minds, often unrecognized, frequently ignored.

The purpose of this book is to maximize your creativity and productivity. You will also increase your ability to solve difficult problems as you get in touch with the powerful insights that are stored deep within the right hemisphere of your brain.

For ninety-five percent of the population, the left side of the brain is the verbal hemisphere. It knows how to work logically and analytically but has little aptitude for imagination or intuitive leaps of insight. These abilities, according to many experts in brain research, are attributes of the right hemisphere.

In our society, the logical, linear skills of the left brain are highly valued, while the more intuitive, artistic skills of the right brain are greatly neglected. The imaginative powers of the right hemisphere have all but atrophied in a high percentage of the adult population; it is possible, however, to develop the latent abilities of the right side of the brain by special mental exercises.

I was first introduced to an awareness of right-brain power by a friend who was the literary critic for the *Los Angeles Times* for twenty-five years, Robert Kirsch. He had devised some imaginative techniques for enhancing his own highly productive work and suggested that I experiment with them as well. Frankly, I was reluctant to spend the time, for the exercises seemed too easy, too entertaining, to have any serious influence on my work. But out of curiosity, I gave them a try. To my surprise, some of his suggestions worked extremely well. I was fascinated by the results and began to modify his suggestions and expand the exercises into a specific program for right-brain stimulation.

I had led workshops in various aspects of creativity since 1970, but when I developed a series of right-brain exercises and presented them in my seminars, I could see what a profound impact they had upon my students. I was especially struck by how quickly the process worked. Creative blocks were broken within hours; tedious ideas gave way to imaginative and exciting concepts. I saw "angels" emerging, where only stone had stood before.

The genesis of some of these right-brain exercises lies thousands of years in the past, originating in various forms of meditation and yoga; others were inspired by psychologists and psychiatrists and experts in biofeedback; still others are based on some of the original suggestions from Robert Kirsch. Many of the exercises are ones I have designed specifically for this program.

Three Questions

In all of my seminars, people want the answers to the same three questions:

1. What is the scientific basis for "The Right-Brain Experience"?
2. How do successful people use right-brain techniques?
3. What difference will this experience make in my life?

These questions established the three-part format for this book. The answers lead you from an intellectual understanding of right-brain functions to an observation of the process and finally, to the creative experience itself.

The first section of this book describes how the right-brain functions in the creative process. Old myths about the elusiveness of creative power are dispelled by new scientific discoveries. Understanding how the hemispheres differ is the first step in knowing how to stimulate the underdeveloped right side of the brain and release the power of this creative hemisphere.

It is not the purpose of this book to elevate the right hemisphere for its sake alone; you want to strengthen the right brain so that it works in better balance with the left. It is this healthy balance between hemispheres that will enable you to function with the maximum power of your whole brain. Also in Part I, you will become familiar with the eleven categories of exercises which I developed to stimulate right-hemisphere activity.

People in widely diverse professions have used right-brain techniques to stimulate creativity, productivity, and problem solving. These techniques have enhanced the careers of men and women in various fields. Eight celebrated achievers allowed me to interview them regarding their insights into the creative process: writers Ray Bradbury and Barbara Goldsmith, cartoonist Charles Schulz, entertainer Steve Allen, counter-espionage agent Ib Melchior, Stanford University Professor of Engineering Robert McKim, designer Cleo Baldon, and dancer/choreographer Marge Champion. These conversations revealed how highly successful and productive people use right-brain techniques in their work. Personal techniques for stimulating imaginative thinking are included in the interviews in Part II.

The third section of "The Right-Brain Experience" is designed as your personal guide book. Within the framework of eleven categories, sixty-seven evocative exercises lead you to discover imaginative powers greater than you ever realized were within you. You will be amazed by the unconscious material that is stimulated by this experience and the direct application this has to your life. The exercises

are fascinating to perform and highly productive. If you want to maximize your creativity and productivity and enhance your capacity for
solving difficult problems, these exercises will enable you to achieve
your goals.

"The Right-Brain Experience" has been constructed as your private seminar. If you were my client, I would suggest that we work
together for two hours a day for six consecutive days. As you adapt
this program to your own life, you may need to move at a slower pace.
But please realize that these exercises have a cumulative effect and
the results are enhanced by daily commitment. For people who are
already deeply in touch with their feelings, creative intensity will occur
after a few exercises. Even for people less in tune with their emotions
this response happens within a few days of embarking on the program.

Through the use of these exercises, you can learn to move easily
into a state of heightened consciousness; *you* can be the one to determine when and how you enter periods of intensified creative power.

A Word of Warning

The right side of the brain is not only the territory of angels and
the Muse but of dragons as well. In this mysterious region of the mind,
you risk stirring the dragons that guard the place where your Muse
dwells. So, a word of warning is only fair.

Dragons sometimes breathe fire and can be dangerous if they
catch us when our defenses are down. There are times when none of
us should try to enter the territory of the unconscious. I would not
recommend that you begin these exercises if you are feeling too emotionally vulnerable to deal with intense feelings. And of course, there
are some people who should never try to stir the unconscious mind
without the help of a therapist. Know yourself and choose wisely—
and be sure to make that decision with the combined judgement of
both sides of your brain.

Beware of anyone who tells you that there is only one way to do
anything. There are people who have been using right-brain techniques for years, never even knowing the term, never using the type
of exercises suggested here. That's because they found other ways to
enter the creative hemisphere of the brain. They have unconsciously
developed their own chisel and hammer to break away the external

edifice of repressive responses that all of us learned during years of "left brain schooling."

If you are one of those people who produces highly creative work, then you have been using other ways of stimulating your unconscious to participate in the creative process. I hope that you will find approaches in this book to enrich your experiences. We can all grow from using a variety of techniques, and these new experiments are designed to help you reach even deeper levels of awareness and productivity.

Many people have had the experience of an intensified creative period with the accompanying feeling of ecstasy. Most people regard it as some mystical or mysterious process they neither understand nor can control. Novelists, and poets especially, often credit this experience to the Muse. The Muse is that mythical creature who lives somewhere in the heavens, who either comes bearing brilliant insights and exquisite metaphors—or else sits tauntingly out of reach.

So much for delusions. The Muse lives within. She inspires not only writers, but painters and scientists, homemakers and business executives. She is shaped by the essence of our personalities and has all the powers of our unconscious minds at her disposal. She lounges in the right hemisphere of the brain—probably appalled by all of the hardened accumulation of "training" that prevents us from setting her free.

The Muse is your friend. This book gives you access to her company. The rest is up to you.

2

Your Logical Brain and Your Intuitive Brain

How It Feels to be Creative

A few years ago, I went into seclusion to work on a theater piece that had to be completed within one month. To my surprise, there was something quite wonderful about working around the clock, taking time only to eat, and sleeping only when I reached a state of exhaustion. When the work was going well, when the words seemed to write themselves and the central character was so real to me that I felt her tears brimming in my eyes, I experienced some physiological changes. Colors were more vivid than before. Familiar music seemed new and full of subtleties I had not remembered. I had no appetite and was aware of a tingling sensation as if there were some aura of energy that stimulated the surface of my skin. Perhaps the closest word I could use to describe the sensation was intense *joy*. The feeling was so exquisite it could hardly be contained. It was as if intuitive insights had embraced conscious awareness and the union was wondrous to experience.

Later, as I was thinking about how I felt during this time, I was puzzled by those physiological sensations. I remembered a sense of abandon, of floating, of flying higher than I had ever been before. Later, I remember joking about "writer's madness"—but now I wondered if others felt that, too, when they were in the midst of intense work. Was this unique to me?

I was reassured when I read *The Courage to Create*, by Rollo

May, for he described similar sensations reported by others during periods of intense creative work. There seems to be a common experience, known to mystics, poets and scientists who encounter the mountain-top experiences. I believe it is the same for all individuals who dare to wander into the territory of the experiential, bearing questions which can only be answered through the wisdom of the unconscious.

If you should feel the inner tremble that comes from a mountain-top experience, savor the moment; be aware of the sensations in your body and enjoy them—this is a rare gift from your right brain. This experience can be so powerful that people have difficulty believing that this feeling of ecstasy comes exclusively from within and is not a "gift from the gods"—or from the Muse.

Once in a great while, people write about the experience of right brain ecstasy. We have come to expect it from poets and philosophers but it can occur to anyone whose work is aided by intuition. Physicist Alan Lightman, writing in *Science 82*, said: "My own christening with doing science on the right side of the brain occurred a decade ago [when] I was a graduate student in physics at Caltech. . . . Other people have tried to describe that lifting feeling when everything suddenly falls into place. For me, the best analogy is what sometimes happens when you're sailing a round bottomed boat in a strong wind. Normally, the hull stays down in the water, with the frictional drag greatly limiting the speed of the boat. But in high wind, every once in a while the hull lifts out of the water, and the drag goes instantly near zero. It feels like a great hand has suddenly grabbed hold and flings you across the surface like a skimming stone. It's called planing.

"I've planed in my scientific career only on a few occasions and then only for a few seconds. Einstein and Darwin probably planed for hours at a time. The years of details at my desk have been bearable because of those moments. I could use a lot more of them."

Dispelling Old Myths

Since ancient times, people have believed the myth that creative inspiration has its source *outside* of the artist. Even today, many creative people are often mystified by the source of their inventive ideas; they feel vulnerable, believing they have no control over the capricious Muse. Some outstanding writers put words to these anxieties:

JOSEPH HELLER: "I don't understand the process of imagination though I know that I am very much at its mercy. I feel like these ideas are floating around in the air and they pick me to settle upon. The ideas come to me. I don't produce them at will."

JAMES DICKEY: "It's really a kind of madness I feel when I'm writing . . . I don't know what it is. . . ."

JOAN DIDION: "There's a lot of mystery to me about writing. . . ."

ERICA JONG: "I don't know where the first line comes from and I don't know who says it to me. It may be the Muse. (I really believe in the Muse, by the way.)"

GORE VIDAL: "I never know what is coming next . . . strange business, all of it. . . ."

Writers, just like other people, seem unable to convoke their own creative powers. They have no explanation for these intense periods of high creativity or for the devastating periods of blocked imaginings.

In the last few years, there have been such great advances in our understanding of creativity that the old myths are now being evaluated in a new light. Many people are discovering that they are not at the mercy of a fickle Muse. They now believe that ideas are floating around in their *heads*, not in the air—for they have learned ways of channeling these ideas at times of their own choosing. They have learned to trust the powers of their unconscious minds and know how to encourage the unconscious to participate in the creative process.

In the Beginning

The desk at which I write this chapter is cluttered with medical journals and research papers. To one side, transcripts of tapes record my meetings with neurologists, psychiatrists, and psychobiologists and form a small mountain of paper. Books lie upon each other like flat stones forming a high wall along the boundaries of my workspace.

No matter which book I open or which paper I read, three names appear with regularity: Sperry, Bogen, and Gazzaniga. Sperry is psychobiologist Roger Sperry of the California Institute of Technology, who won the 1981 Nobel Prize for Physiology and Medicine for his "split-brain" studies on the functions of the two hemispheres of the brain. Under Sperry's guidance, his student Michael Gazzaniga carried out the testing of the patients, while neurosurgeon Joseph Bogen conducted neurological tests and, with Phillip Vogel, performed the first "split-brain" surgery. These men—working with many others—are responsible for the first insights into the differences between the left and right hemispheres of the brain. Split-brain research on human subjects began in the 1960's at the California Institute of Technology. Scientists, who had been working on split-brain studies on animals since the 1950's, finally had the unique opportunity to test a human subject. "W.J." was a soldier in World War II. He had parachuted behind enemy lines, was taken prisoner and sent to a P.O.W. camp where he was hit in the head by a rifle butt. The wound damaged his brain to such an extent that it caused devastating seizures that made normal life impossible.

W.J. had not responded to medical efforts to improve his intractable epilepsy, so as a last ditch effort, doctors decided that he was to be the first split-brain patient. The plan was this: the neurosurgeons would cut the *corpus callosum*, a mass of nerve fibers which bridged the hemispheres and allowed W.J.'s seizures to transfer from one side of the brain to the other. That surgery, known as a commissurotomy, would leave each hemisphere isolated so that when seizures occurred in the damaged hemisphere, they could not spread to the other side. This would reduce the severity of the seizures and the patient could then be treated with medication. If everything went as planned, W.J. would be able to lead a more normal life. The surgery was successful and soon another patient, and then ten others, were helped by this radical procedure. The long span of research continues to this day; the same patients still return periodically to Cal Tech to allow researchers to study the effects of the surgeries.

The Discovery

What those split-brain researchers discovered is that the *corpus callosum* is the communications network which sends information back and forth between the two hemispheres of the brain. When the *corpus callosum* has been severed, one side of the brain cannot communicate with the other. It is as if, within every person, two separate minds were operating. Without the help of the *corpus callosum*, each "mind" functions separately and has no idea what is happening inside its partner. With the mental experience of each hemisphere in isolation, researchers were able to study the separate functions of each side of a single brain. Through sophisticated testing procedures, they worked to determine which tasks are performed by the left hemisphere and which are performed by the right. (For the testing procedures used, see Notes.)

Researchers discovered that each side of the brain has its own area of specialization and processes information in its own way. Subsequent tests have shown that in a normally functioning brain, the *corpus callosum* enables both hemispheres to work together for almost every activity, although one hemisphere or the other will predominate for a specific task.

New Insights into Creativity

Of the three men whose work with split-brain patients revolutionized current medical thinking about the human brain, only Joseph Bogen addressed himself to the subject of creativity. At present, a dozen or more names have become associated with the application of this new research to the creative process.

In ninety-five percent of the population, it is the left hemisphere that remembers names, adds columns of numbers, computes time and works in a logical, linear fashion. The right hemisphere is the mysterious, artistic side of the brain where metaphors are understood and emotions are realized. It's where dreams and imagery occur and fantasies are born.

When an artist instinctively knows how to balance color and line, when jazz musicians wail in concert, when a writer begins a scene and can almost hear the characters speak their lines, it is the right hemisphere of the brain that directs their course. In the right hemisphere, the seeds of passion and creativity are stored.

We live in a society that shows most respect for people who are "left-brain dominant." The left-brain–dominant schoolgirl who remembers names, adds numbers properly, and works with a great sense of order and tidiness is praised and gets a star beside her name. The right-brain–dominant child who daydreams and stares at distant clouds, preferring to make up stories rather than learn her lesson, is sent home with a disciplinary note.

Most children learn early that conformity and retention are more praiseworthy than creativity.

Just as a muscle will atrophy from lack of use, the right hemisphere of the brain also suffers when its use isn't encouraged. Even though these creative gifts may be underdeveloped, that doesn't mean they can't be revived. The first step in restoring the full power of the right brain is to learn what to expect from each hemisphere.

Left-Brain Specialization

Your left brain is your *logical* hemisphere. Until recently, doctors called this your "dominant" hemisphere. But in fact, your left hemisphere is only dominant for the following tasks:

Verbal: The left hemisphere is the side of your brain that is involved in language skills. This is the side that controls speech, that is able to read and write. It remembers facts, recalls names and dates, and knows how to spell.

Analytical: The left hemisphere is your logical, analytical side. It can evaluate factual material in a rational way.

Literal: Your left brain understands only the most literal interpretation of words.

Linear: Information is processed sequentially by the left brain. This is a one-step-at-a-time way of thinking.

Mathematical: Numbers and symbols are comprehended in the left hemisphere. The logical, analytical thinking required for the working of advanced mathematical problems is produced by the expertise of your left brain.

Controls movements on the opposite side of the body: If you wiggle your *right* thumb, it is your *left* brain that gave the instructions.

Right-Brain Specialization

The right brain is your intuitive hemisphere. Although it is frequently called the non-dominant hemisphere, the right brain is dominant for the following types of activity:

Non-verbal: Right-brain knowledge is not achieved through words but through images.

Holistic (non-linear): The right hemisphere can process many kinds of information simultaneously, sees problems holistically, and can make great leaps of insight. It is able to evaluate the whole problem at once. The right brain recognizes faces, seeing the features "as a whole."

Spatial: Visuospatial functions—those involving perceptions of location and spatial relationships—are processes of the right hemisphere. Your right brain knows how to work jigsaw puzzles and enables you to find your way around your house without getting lost.

Musical: Innate musical talent, as well as the ability to respond to music, are right brain functions (although extensive musical education will result in left hemisphere involvement, as well).

Metaphoric: Your right brain understands metaphors and imagery. It can change the literal meaning of a sentence into its connotations: If someone says, "He's really on my back," the right brain knows the difference between what is said and what is meant.

Imaginative: Your right brain is capable of fantasy; it makes up stories and dreams and knows how to play. It is also the hemisphere that is speculative and imaginative. The right brain wonders, "What if . . ."

Artistic: Drawing, painting, and sculpting are natural talents of the right hemisphere.

Emotional: Although emotions are actually a product of another part of the brain (the limbic system), it is the right hemisphere that is more in touch with these feelings.

Sexual: Making love is a right hemisphere experience—unless you're trying too hard or are overly concerned with technique.

Spiritual: It is the right hemisphere that is involved in worship, prayer, and mysticism.

Dream maker: Dreams are primarily a function of the right side of the brain. It is your imaginative, metaphoric internal-poet that creates dream images.

Controls Movement on the Opposite Side of the Body: If you wiggle your *left* thumb, it is your *right* brain that gave the instruction.

The Other Five Percent

The preceding breakdown of hemispheric specialization is valid for ninety-five percent of the population. This includes practically all right-handed people. Specialization in lefthanders, who compose about ten percent of the population, is less clearly defined. Most are specialized in the same way as righthanders; some have "mixed dominance" (meaning some language skills and some spatial skills are in each hemisphere). Left-handed people who have left-handed mothers may even have reversed specialization (i.e., language skills would be on the right side and spatial on the left). Even if you are a part of the five percent of the population that's not clearly lateralized, the exercises in Part III of this book will be helpful in stimulating the part of your brain that is specialized in imaginative thinking.

Development of the Hemispheres

The specialization of the hemispheres seems to be unique to human maturity. Other primates and very young human children show little, if any, hemispheric specialization. In fact, a small child can lose an entire hemisphere and still grow up with normal intelligence, because each side does possess the *potential* for both modes. But after the age of five, the loss of a hemisphere will result in a permanent impairment. (Most researchers think the specialization of the hemispheres is related to the acquisition of language.)

One of the most delightful clarifications of how the hemispheres contribute to our choices is seen in the magazine ad for Saab automobiles. "A Car For Your Left Brain" and "A Car For Your Right Brain" (shown on the next two pages) is entertaining and informative . . . even if you're not in the market for a new car.

The Perfect Partnership

When the hemispheres function properly, the cooperation between them is a perfect partnership. There is harmony in their goals and they avoid getting in each other's way. Each is supportive of the other and each does what it does best. They complement each other in almost all activities.

- The poet draws upon the right hemisphere for deep feelings and an understanding of imagery and metaphors, but the left hemisphere finds the words to fit those emotions and insights.

- An architect uses his right brain to conceive the spatial relationships with the aesthetic mood he wants to create. But his left brain will deal with dimensions and stresses and building codes.

- A scientist needs his skilled left brain for deductive reasoning. But it is the intuitive right brain that often leads him to that leap of insight that solves a complex problem.

A CAR FOR THE LEFT SIDE OF YOUR BRAIN.

The left side of your brain, recent investigations tell us, is the logical side.

It figures out that $1 + 1 = 2$. And, in a few cases, that $E = mc^2$.

On a more mundane level, it chooses the socks you wear, the cereal you eat, and the car you drive. All by means of rigorous Aristotelian logic.

However, and a big however it is, for real satisfaction, you must achieve harmony with the other side of your brain.

The right side, the poetic side, that says, "Yeah, Car X has a reputation for lasting a long time but it's so dull, who'd want to drive it that long anyway?"

The Saab Turbo looked at from all sides.

To the left side of your brain, Saab turbocharging is a technological feat that retains good gas mileage while also increasing performance.

To the right side of your brain, Saab turbocharging is what makes a Saab go like a bat out of hell.

The left side sees the safety in high performance. (Passing on a two-lane highway. Entering a freeway in the midst of high-speed traffic.)

The right side lives only for the thrills.

The left side considers that *Road & Track* magazine just named Saab "The Sports Sedan for the Eighties." By unanimous choice of its editors.

The right side eschews informed endorsements by editors who have spent a lifetime comparing cars. The right side doesn't know much about cars, but knows what it likes.

The left side scans this chart.

Wheelbase	99.1 inches
Length	187.6 inches
Width	66.5 inches
Height	55.9 inches
Fuel-tank capacity	16.6 gallons
EPA City	19 mpg *
EPA Highway	31 mpg *

The right side looks at the picture on the opposite page.

The left side compares a Saab's comfort with that of a Mercedes. Its performance with that of a BMW. Its braking with that of an Audi.

The right side looks at the picture.

The left side looks ahead to the winter when a Saab's front-wheel drive will keep a Saab in front of traffic.

The right side looks at the picture.

The left side also considers the other seasons of the year when a Saab's front-wheel drive gives it the cornering ability of a sports car.

The right side looks again at the picture.

Getting what you need vs. getting what you want.

Needs are boring; desires are what make life worth living.

The left side of your brain is your mother telling you that a Saab is good for you. "Eat your vegetables." (In today's world, you need a car engineered like a Saab.) "Put on your raincoat." (The Saab is economical. Look at the price-value relationship.) "Do your homework." (The passive safety of the construction. The active safety of the handling.)

1982 SAAB PRICE** LIST		
900 3-Door	5-Speed	$10,400
	Automatic	10,750
900 4-Door	5-Speed	$10,700
	Automatic	11,050
900S 3-Door	5-Speed	$12,100
	Automatic	12,450
900S 4-Door	5-Speed	$12,700
	Automatic	13,050
900 Turbo 3-Door	5-Speed	$15,600
	Automatic	15,950
900 Turbo 4-Door	5-Speed	$16,260
	Automatic	16,610
All turbo models include a Sony XR70, 4-Speaker Stereo Sound System as standard equipment. The stereo can be, of course, perfectly balanced: left and right.		

The right side of your brain guides your foot to the clutch, your hand to the gears, and listens for the "zzzooommm."

Together, they see the 1982 Saab Turbo as the responsible car the times demand you get. And the performance car you've always, deep down, wanted with half your mind.

*Saab 900 Turbo. Remember, use estimated mpg for comparison only. Mileage varies with speed, trip length, and weather. Actual highway mileage will probably be less. **Manufacturer's suggested retail price. Not including taxes, license, freight, dealer charges or options desired by either side of your brain.

Most creative work requires the combined abilities of intuitive awareness and logical thinking.

It is important to remember that the hemispheres function together in almost every activity, but that they process information differently, and the intensity of involvement of each depends upon the specific task.

When Partners Are at War

In business partnerships, when one partner gets too aggressive and tries to take over the role of the other person, the result is usually disastrous. The brain has similar problems with partnership; the left hemisphere often becomes too assertive, trying to solve everything with its logical deductions. Sometimes that hemisphere is so aggressive that it tries to do jobs that are best accomplished by the right side of the brain. When that happens, the brain's partnership is in trouble.

If a person relies too heavily on the left hemisphere, he may lose the intuitive powers of the right side of his brain; he may even deny that those powers exist, for he is too far removed from an awareness of his unconscious to even feel its presence. That person usually has trouble in personal relationships, for the contribution of the more sensitive right brain is needed for harmonious interaction with others.

Many people use the less proficient hemisphere for a task at hand. Some activities obviously require the right or the left brain, but a great many activities could really be performed by either the intuitive right brain or the analytical left. In that unclaimed territory, many conflicts arise. Most of us tend to rely on one approach or the other out of habit, rather than from a clear understanding of which hemisphere is best suited for the job. Only in the last few years have researchers indicated that conscious effort to stimulate a specific hemisphere can alter performance.

Since the first split-brain case, there has been a deluge of information in medical journals about "cerebral lateralization" (i.e., the specialized functions of each hemisphere). Researchers often disagree about some of the findings and each scientific paper comes with a list of references of other studies which will validate their own. (They are a meticulous crowd, these scientists; I was particularly impressed by Joseph Bogen's synopsis, "The Other Side of the Brain," which included no less than 382 references!)

As a layperson in this field, I tried to find the highest ledge of surety in this rising sea of information. Jay Myers, who is currently studying the split-brain cases at Cal Tech, directed me in finding out about the latest research in the field. And because my interest in the brain is for the sake of the creative process, I sought out the only psychiatrist who worked with the early split-brain cases. Klaus Hoppe, M.D., a psychoanalyst in Los Angeles, graciously consented to several interviews regarding his work in hemispheric lateralization.

Because dreams are reported to be a function of the right hemisphere, it came as quite a surprise to learn from Dr. Hoppe that he saw a patient whose right hemisphere had been surgically removed, yet she reported a dream! But then he went on to say that the dream was missing all proper "dream work." The dream had none of the usual components of normal dreams.

Hoppe called his patient "Mrs. G" and said she was a 32-year-old former singer and actress. At first she told him that she could not remember any dreams or fantasies at all. Finally, she reported that she had dreamed that "Dr. Bogen and a psychologist drove her in the latter's Volkswagen to a restaurant and treated her to lobster and martinis—exactly as it had happened in reality a short while before." Her single reported dream came very close to reality and lacks the characteristics usually associated with dreaming.

A Hypothetical Case

I would like to condense the scientific findings generally attributed to each hemisphere by presenting an extreme hypothetical case: imagine that two men in their early thirties are in a hospital where they have undergone brain surgery. The surgery is called a hemispherectomy. One person had his left hemisphere removed and the other had his right hemisphere removed.

Prior to surgery, both people were sharply lateralized (strongly right-handed and left-brain verbal) with no individual variation from the norm. The remaining hemisphere of each person is assumed to function properly, but it has not learned how to compensate for the missing partner.

Patient #1 sits on the edge of his bed. Only a week before, the entire right hemisphere of his brain was removed because of a tumor. His left brain is intact and functioning normally. We will call him Left-Brain Larry.

Patient #2, who shares the same room, is sitting in the chair, staring out the window. Because of a tumor, this patient has undergone the removal of his entire left hemisphere. His right hemisphere is functioning appropriately and we will call him Right-Brain Rick.

Now imagine that you are involved in follow-up studies of hemispherectomy patients. You enter the room to observe these two men and find the following situation. (Remember, each hemisphere controls the movements of the *opposite* side of the body.)

Larry's functioning left brain enables him to move the right side of his body without difficulty. He holds a cup of coffee in his right hand and shifts the position of his right leg. "Do you want cream for your coffee?" you ask him, and he says, "No, thank you." The tone of his voice is flat, lacking expression. A paper is beside him on the bed and you notice that he looks over and scans the headlines. If you asked him to, he would be able to work math problems as well as he could before the surgery.

But as you talk further with Larry, you see the devastating effects of his surgery. Because he has no right brain, he is totally paralyzed on the left side of his body. Although he has been able to carry on a conversation with you, his responses are sometimes quite strange. He is absolutely literal. "How do you feel?" you ask, and he answers, "With my hands." Larry has lost the capacity for imaginative thinking and for intuitive leaps of insight.

You help Larry into a wheelchair and move him into a corridor for a change of scene. He has no idea where he is in relation to his room, for he has lost all visuospatial organizational abilities. Realizing that, you know he will not be able to work a jigsaw puzzle or put together a child's toy. He is unable to dress himself without assistance; he wouldn't know that the sleeves of his shirt had any relationship to his arms.

Suddenly, two people in the corridor begin to shout at each other. Left-Brain Larry understands the words but shows no response to the emotions behind the words. He doesn't respond to his wife's tears and words of compassion. He isn't even depressed by his surgery, for the normal response of sorrow is outside of his left-brain capabilities.

Back in his room, you ask if he would like to hear some music; you turn on the radio and realize that he is totally indifferent to the melody. A close friend comes into the room but Larry doesn't seem to realize who he is, for his remaining hemisphere has difficulty recognizing faces at a glance.

Ask him if he dreams, and he will probably tell you that he does not. If he does say that he dreams, and you ask him to tell you about it, he will probably describe something that actually happened not long ago.

And what of Patient #2? He has been sitting in a chair all this time, watching you. You notice, immediately, that only the left side of his body moves as he shifts position in the chair. But you are also aware of his sadness. In an effort to comfort him, you smile and tell him that he is looking better. Although he can't speak, you think he understands what you said. His wife enters the room, and he immediately recognizes her and looks pleased by her simple words of affection. She has brought a small portable stereo with her, and he enjoys the music. When the song ends, Right-Brain Rick, who cannot find the words to say his own name or express his basic needs, shocks everyone by beginning suddenly to *sing a hymn* he learned in early childhood. You praise him for being able to sing the words well enough for you to understand them and encourage him to try other songs. But Rick's right brain has only retained the simple lyrics he learned many years before. However, he can *recite by rote* the words to a simple prayer he learned when he was a very young boy. And to his wife's amazement, he is still able to swear—apparently the visceral language has made an impact on his emotional right hemisphere. Except for these three conditions he is totally aphasic.

You bring out a jigsaw puzzle to entertain Rick and he has no difficulty putting it together. Later, as you move his wheelchair down the hall, he seems to know exactly where he is and shows no signs of disorientation.

Right-Brain Rick can neither read nor work arithmetic problems but he likes for you to read poetry to him, and a dream researcher tells you that last night he observed Rick's rapid eye movements (REM), which indicate that he is experiencing dreams.

You have made careful notes of the behavior of these two men and the abilities you have observed. You probably wonder if they retained other abilities you haven't yet recognized. The most obvious conclusion you draw from these patients is that each half of the brain functions in a highly specialized way that is dramatic in its uniqueness.

You have just seen the innate aptitudes of each hemisphere demonstrated in an extreme hypothetical situation.

The Adaptive Brain

The human body has an enormous potential to recover from injury. It is possible that in the weeks and months after surgery, a patient with a hemispherectomy will be able to develop some small latent abilities of the remaining hemisphere. Early in life, considerable recovery after such an operation can be expected. (Researchers differ as to how old a child can be and still retain an ability to recover: some say before age 5, others say before puberty, still others say age 20.) In older patients, recovery is so minimal that normal cognitive functions cannot be regained.

An Ancient Awareness

Long before scientists advanced the concept of brain hemisphere specialization, ancient peoples were intuitively aware of it. In various cultures throughout the world, the left side of the body (controlled by the right brain) is associated with mystery and emotion. The right side (controlled by the left brain) is associated with properness and morality. William Domhoff, in a study on the myth and symbolism of left and right notes that the left hand (right brain) is usually associated with taboo, the sacred, the unconscious, the feminine, the intuitive and the dreamer. The right hand (left brain), he found, is associated with propriety, goodness, masculinity and logic. The Hopi Indians of the American Southwest distinguished the use of the two hands: the right for writing, the left for making music. Arabs use the left hand for bathroom functions, the right hand for eating. Our ancestors thought that witches were left-handed. The earliest sign of a saint was that in infancy he would refuse the left breast. Girls were believed to come from the semen of the left testicle; boys from the semen of the right.

Hippocrates is thought to be the first to report that there was a difference between one side of the brain and the other. This observation came about when soldiers who received sword wounds to the right side of their heads would show the effect on the left side of their bodies, while wounds to the left side of their brains influenced movement on the right side of the body. And because of this he concluded that, "The brain of man is double."

It was almost two thousand years before much interest was shown in Hippocrates' observation. In 1861, a young French physician, Paul

Broca, noticed a correlation between damage to the left side of the brain and loss of speech, a condition he called aphasia.

From then on, doctors took a keen interest in the brain and its functions. They began to observe the differences between patients who had strokes and tumors on the left side and those who had them on the right. They observed patients who had undergone removal of one hemisphere of the brain and realized how striking the differences really were. But it was not until the famous "split-brain" surgeries of the 1960's (those that involved severing the *corpus callosum*) that scientists were able to contrast the abilities of *each* hemisphere within one individual, testing first the left brain and then the right brain. This isolation of the hemispheres within one person has provided a major source of information for how the hemispheres differ.

The Controversy

Scientific studies that challenge old and established assumptions are always received with skepticism. But, in defense of those who disagree with the current findings, it must be stated that research on the brain has only begun to reveal how the hemispheres function. The brain has been a mystery since the beginning of time and it will remain a mystery for many years to come. Not in your lifetime or in mine will all the answers be found. We are at the start of a long road and must keep in mind that there will undoubtedly be some conflicting assumptions until many years of research studies present uncontestable conclusions. It is best to use qualifiers when talking about people and their brain functions so I rely heavily on the words "most," "usually," and "rarely."

In his Nobel lecture, Dr. Roger Sperry said, "The more we learn, the more complex becomes the picture for predictions regarding any one individual and the more it seems to reinforce the conclusion that the kind of unique individuality in our brain networks makes that of fingerprints or facial features appear gross and simple by comparison."

Medical research moves slowly. Fortunately for us, the information that has been reported has enabled researchers in the behavioral sciences to apply these findings to creativity. If you are interested in learning more about the scientific findings, you will find the Notes and Bibliography sections of this book most helpful.

The exercise program in this book evolved from scientific knowledge about the hemispheres of the brain, but this research is only the background for this program. Whatever future discoveries advance neurological thinking, these exercises stand independent of the medical framework and enable people, with or without scientific backgrounds, to expand their creativity.

3

The Key to
Increased Creativity

To get maximum benefit from this book, it is important that you understand the specific purpose of each of the exercises in this six-day program. Why do they work? What do they do? How do they stimulate the right hemisphere? The following pages will provide some answers to these questions and give you a *left*-brain understanding of their functions. But it is only when your right brain has experienced these exercises, in Part III, that you will fully comprehend their power.

You may be familiar with some of the techniques in this program. Many of them have their origin in various forms of meditation, biofeedback, psychiatry, psychology, and related fields. What is unique in "The Right-Brain Experience" is the synthesis of the various techniques. These exercises draw from the most valuable tools of each discipline. From meditation, you will become familiar with aids for relaxation and concentration that encourage spontaneity and intuition. From the field of psychology come valuable insights on how childhood memories and sensory stimulation can be used to trigger emotions for use in solving current problems. You will learn how to make your dreams work for you in concrete ways, as you employ techniques from psychiatrists as well as from an enlightened tribe of aborigines in the Malay Peninsula. Experts in a wide variety of fields have developed ideas that I have gathered like rare gems from the far corners of the earth to use for my own purposes.

Although many techniques from psychology are used in the exercises, the program does not have self-analysis as its goal: Therapeutic insights that might be gotten are a serendipity of this book. The goals in doing these exercises are clearly defined: Each category has been devised to lead you directly toward achievements in creativity and productivity.

When you finish this chapter and thoroughly understand each of the eleven categories of exercises, you will recognize similar patterns used by the outstanding achievers interviewed in Part II. When you see how these creative people have learned to make use of the right-brain potential, you will be better prepared to trust the right-brain process and enjoy the experience. On each of the six days, you will do one exercise in each of the following eleven categories. (One bonus exercise is presented on the first day.) Each succeeding exercise is designed to lead you deeper into the territory of the right hemisphere.

Category 1.
Outsmarting the Left Brain

People are most receptive to right-brain insights when the body is relaxed and the mind is free from internal chatter. Therefore, the first two exercises in this program are warm-up exercises to help you reach a receptive mental and physical state as you begin.

You may remember seeing a cross-section of a twig or a snowflake under a microscope. Those images are examples of mandalas—geometric patterns formed by a series of concentric forms around one focal point. Mandalas are also found in the design of the human eye: the pupil forms the center and around it the iris completes the symmetrical pattern. You will also find mandalas in gemstones, in flowers, and in seeds.

Mandalas have been used for centuries by mystics to increase concentration and to achieve a mental state receptive to spiritual enlightenment.

Symmetrical design is also found in art, architecture, and religious symbols. Its form is implicitly harmonious and, in many cases, exquisite in design. Hold a kaleidoscope to your eye and watch the changing forms of the mandala. Artists have used it in a myriad of ways: in cloisonné jewelry, in paintings, in pottery designs (especially in the

Orient). Psychologist Carl Jung used the mandala as a tool in his own psychological growth and he incorporated mandalas in therapy techniques with his patients. He reported its recurrent presence in dreams and believed that mandalas had a significance that went beyond the individual dreamer's own experiences.

Churches and cathedrals throughout Europe and America incorporate mandalas in the stained glass windows that have been exalted by artists and worshippers for centuries.

In this warm-up exercise you will spend a few minutes concentrating on the center of a mandala, relaxing your left hemisphere and letting your spatially-expert right hemisphere take over.

The most effective way to use the mandala in this right-brain program is to sit in a quiet place, in a comfortable position, with the conscious intention of reaching a state of relaxation and concentration. As you focus on the center of the mandala, you will begin to relax. As you concentrate on the visual pattern for five minutes or more, a quieting of the mind will gradually replace your usual inner dialogue. After a few sessions of using the mandala in this way, you will discover that worries and extraneous thoughts are unable to penetrate your consciousness.

If you are unfamiliar with the use of the mandala, you may be skeptical of how staring at a simple pattern can produce such changes in your mental mode. Science has suggested recently a direct connection between the ability to respond to spatial configurations, such as the simple mandala, and the right hemisphere's function. Your brain produces different wave patterns depending on the type of activity in which it is engaged. In response to this intense focusing on a simple pattern, your brain will begin to produce slow alpha patterns. Alpha patterns can be measured by biofeedback detectors and they indicate a relaxed condition in one or both hemispheres.

Although the left brain cannot cope with spatial relationships, it may try to retain control of the brain by analyzing the pattern in terms of squares and circles and crosses. You can keep this from happening by concentrating on the center of the pattern and trying to see as much of the peripheral design as possible *without analyzing it*. Soon the left brain will acquiesce to the powers of the right brain. In effect, the mandala is being used to outsmart the left hemisphere so that you can shift to the right-brain mode.

Category 2.
Biofeedback Training

The biofeedback exercises offer a mind-over-body process to help you relax physically. This will enable you to be more receptive to suggestions from your right hemisphere.

About five years ago, I went to see Melvyn Werbach, M.D., who was the director of Clinical Biofeedback at UCLA's Pain Control Unit, and is now Director of the Biofeedback Medical Clinic in Beverly Hills. I wanted help with a physical problem: migraine headaches. An unexpected benefit from my visits was that I learned a procedure that would be an invaluable tool for the creative process.

Dr. Werbach taped electrodes onto my fingers and to the muscles near my spine. These wires were attached to a biofeedback machine. Lights began to flash on the machine; a beeping sound indicated that my anxiety had been transmitted from my mind to my body, and the wires of this remarkable machine were "feeding back," by means of light and sound, the information my body was emitting. I could actually *see* and *hear* the tension that was troubling me.

The doctor then taught me some methods of deep breathing and other basic relaxation techniques. He also introduced me to the use of imagery as a tool for relaxation. My suspicion of the entire process only increased the blinking and beeping of the machine. I remember complaining that this wasn't working (and thinking that it never would). But, gradually, as I "gave up" and "quit trying" (which are two important steps in the process), I could see the lights flashing only intermittently and the beeping noise soon became silent. Any anxious thought, however, would make the machine light up and beep again. By quieting the mind and the body, I could cause the machine to be quiet. While still connected to the machine and in a state of deep relaxation, I gradually learned to release the tension in my back muscles and regulate blood circulation by consciously raising the temperature of my hands by several degrees. Through the entire procedure, the biofeedback machine continued to report on my progress.

From a medical standpoint, the treatments were successful: Five years later, the migraine headaches are still approximately eighty-five percent under control. But the treatments had other permanent effects. The deep relaxation, which is so valuable for creative work and for sustained productivity, was now something over which I had a new kind of control.

I also discovered that the richness of the imagery of my "mind's eye" was enhanced considerably while I was in this state of deep relaxation. As I lay there with eyes closed, images moved across my mind in colors I never knew existed. I began to enjoy imagining abstract forms as I moved from normal consciousness into an altered state of awareness. As my left brain relaxed and I felt the shift to the right hemisphere, I experienced the sensation of floating, of soaring, of feeling incredibly peaceful and confident. Since the slow alpha waves are produced by both hemispheres of the brain, the value of deep relaxation is not exclusive to the right side. In fact, this altered state may work as an equalizer, creating a condition where the hemispheres can rest easily together. From this starting point of equality, the right hemisphere has a better chance of asserting its power.

I quickly saw that the applications of what I had learned with Dr. Werbach could extend far beyond any immediate physical situation. My writing was definitely better when I was in this deeply relaxed condition. After a few hours, of course, that nice, easy feeling would wear off and I found I was again tensing both body and mind. So I devised a plan: I would develop a practical way to use this new state of awareness in the normal routine of the day.

Many of the relaxation exercises in this program are the same ones I learned from Dr. Werbach. Others have been expanded to include techniques from yoga and autogenics, and other meditative concepts. Even without feedback from a machine, the exercises will effect tremendous changes in your body and mind. Perhaps the feedback you will get is from your own increased creativity.

Category 3. Guided Imagery

When you visit a foreign country where English is not understood, it's a good idea to familiarize yourself with the language or else have a bilingual guide. Otherwise, it is very difficult to explain your needs and to receive answers to your questions. If you don't understand the meaning of the words, you have to rely on your ability to interpret facial expressions, to hear the implications in the tone of voice, to read gestures and body language. It's also helpful to be intuitive and highly resourceful.

If your trip was to take you into the territory of your right brain, you would need to use those same techniques to understand what was going on. The right-brain way of "knowing" is not through words but through images, metaphors, and symbolism. Learning to communicate in those terms is not at all difficult once you make the decision to try.

Imagery is the visual picture your mind creates in reverie and in dreams. As you learn how to interpret this visual language, you will have access to important right-brain communication.

In this third category of exercises, I will lead you into specific situations where you are asked to use your right-brain aptitude for imagery. After you have relaxed your left hemisphere through the use of the mandala and the biofeedback techniques, you are ready to move deeper into a right-brain mode of experience. As I lead you to imagine places and experiences that may seem unfamiliar, you will find that your own creative powers begin to express themselves. Your mind will create vivid images; smells and tastes and sensations of touch will suddenly become an integral part of your fantasy. Feelings that are often intense and sometimes exquisitely pleasurable will emerge with the imagery.

If this is your first experience with guided imagery, you will probably be astonished by the power of your mind to evoke such vivid scenes and intense feelings. It is more powerful than daydreaming; it is more controllable than dreams. This is not the reality of left-brain consciousness; it is the reality of right-brain experience—which is just as valid as left-brain logical thinking.

During some of these guided-imagery exercises, you will be able to create an "inner advisor." This imaginary character resides in your unconscious and is the personification of all your right-brain wisdom. This "person" has access to every feeling and event you have ever experienced and will give you advice that can positively influence personal and professional decisions.

You can speak freely with this Wise and Loving Person about the most intimate longings of your soul. You may be aware that some of these desires are in conflict with your left-brain logical self. The Wise Person will help you understand your needs and will accept whatever you feel without condemnation.

If you are a musician, you can ask that Wise Person to sing for you and ask that the song be original and as beautiful as any song you have ever heard. Later, when you write it down, you will know that the music is truly your own, for it came from the deepest regions of your mind.

If you are a businessperson, you might want to talk with this Wise Person about a specific conflict. You may need to see the "whole" of the problem more clearly or you may want to get insights into your deepest feelings about the problem.

If you are struggling with a personal matter involving your emotions, the Wise Person is perfectly able to help you clarify your feelings. I am not suggesting that your intuitive hemisphere is always right: but it will tell you the point of view of your *feeling* self. Later, you can compare the suggestions of the Wise Person of your inner self with your analytical, logical self and make a decision based on your whole-brain expertise.

Guided imagery is not only a technique used for stimulating creativity, it has also found acceptance with medical doctors in fields ranging from psychotherapy to oncology. Although the exercises in this book are definitely not intended for medical application, it may be interesting to know that doctors use imagery for healing.

For instance, Bruce Christianson, M.D., a psychiatrist in Los Angeles, told me he uses imagery and inner advisors with specific patients. He finds it helpful to teach his patients to use self-hypnosis to experience a lessening of anxieties and to get in touch with the deeper awareness of the right hemisphere. Self-hypnosis is another way of enabling one to experience imagery, and the processes can be used together with great success.

Dr. Christianson, who was trained at the Mayo Clinic and has a Freudian analytic background, said, "I think the use of imagery and other right-brain techniques is 'the way of the future' for psychotherapy. I have found it to be a much faster procedure than conventional therapies and it involves less dependency on the therapist."

Guided imagery and intense fantasizing are used as primary tools at the UCLA Pain Control Unit which was pioneered by Dr. David Bresler. In his book, *Free Yourself from Pain*, Dr. Bresler strongly advocates the use of guided imagery and the "inner advisor" as a technique of dealing with chronic pain. "I'm teaching people to do what I would have had them committed for doing ten years ago" he wrote, referring to the conversation with imaginary advisors. But he adds, "Patients report that they're getting relief using guided imagery and it does appear to be totally safe when properly used. Keep in mind that the autonomic nervous system, which regulates pain and pleasure, is controlled by the unconscious mind. By communicating effectively with the right hemisphere, you may be able to produce dramatic changes in your body."

O. Carl Simonton, M.D., a radiation oncologist in Fort Worth, Texas, has developed a unique program for his cancer patients. He uses guided imagery to help them visualize their bodies becoming well. This unique approach to healing, *used in conjunction with more conventional treatments*, has resulted in cancer remissions far in excess of normal statistics.

Right-brain techniques offer new therapies to the medical community; they are highly praised by some doctors and scoffed at by others. But patients who have used the techniques, and have had successful results, are overwhelmingly enthusiastic about a medical procedure that does not involve the use of pain-killing drugs.

Category 4.
Transitional Objects

A transitional object is some item from early childhood, such as a baby blanket or teddy bear, that helps a young child build a personal identity and be less dependent on its mother. The exercises in this category will help you search your memory for specific objects from your childhood that had particular significance in your early life. Recalling these objects opens the door to extensive recall of emotions and events from that period of time. A transitional object may be a tangible item, although it can even be a sensory recollection. A psychiatrist who was my private client, for instance, recalled a particular smell that he associated with his grandmother's house and the nourishing spirit she brought to his life.

Is there one specific memory of a tangible object from your childhood that has particular meaning to you? Think for a moment, and see if anything comes to mind. In these exercises involving transitional objects, you will learn to use recollections as tools for mature creative endeavor. Most high achievers are well integrated with the "inner child" and many of these people keep tangible transitional objects around them as a source of instant recall for nourishing and challenging memories. But, whether you invoke memories of the past so that you can understand their influence upon your life, or whether you invoke those memories as grist for the mill of creative expression, they are important parts of your inner self and worthy of attention and concern.

Usually memory provides only the pale shadow of a past experience—a snatch of conversation, an echo of the emotion from a memory that is stirred but remains obscure. But when the right hemisphere of the brain is in control of your experience, you can allow yourself to remember those events almost as if you were reliving them. You should be wary, however, of stirring up traumatic memories. These should be explored only with expert help. But I do encourage you to encounter enriching experiences—even some that make you feel vulnerable. Recapturing sensitive feelings is the first step toward integrating your inner child into your adult life and is essential to most forms of creativity.

Some people have chosen not to remember their early lives. It is as if the option to forget has been exercised so often that their vivid memory is damaged. The past is not lost to you, however, if you *want* to remember. Lawrence Kubie, a neurologist and Freudian analyst, writes of an experience he conducted with patients under hypnosis. Prior to hypnosis, the subjects were brought into a room and allowed to stay there only a few minutes. When they came out and were asked to describe as many things in the room as they could, they would usually name twenty or thirty items. Under hypnosis, they would go into the room and come out to make a list of two hundred things they could remember in that room.

You do not have to be under hypnotic inducement to uncover many buried memories which will enrich your life. The right-brain techniques in this book will effectively evoke specific instances that can be useful for your creative inspiration and for unique approaches to solving current difficulties.

Category 5.
"Other" Hand Writing

What possible benefit could come from writing with your "other" hand? It will probably make you feel awkward; the words may be hard to read, or perhaps impossible to read, and the very silliness of it may make you resist doing it. But, just as the right side of the brain controls the movement of the left hand, the converse is also true. Writing with the left hand, at strategic moments during this program, can encourage unconscious material to surface.

When my clients are stuck on a problem, I suggest they write about the problem with their usual writing-hand and then I ask them to answer specific questions by writing with the other hand. After some embarrassed laughter, the words start to come and they are frequently amazed at what the other hand writes. Painters have often found this technique valuable, and many art teachers suggest that students paint with the other hand for a while. When they switch back to the usual hand, the students discover that their work is freer and more spontaneous. Writers use this simple technique to break through minor blocks with images or metaphors. You can use this any time you are in a right-brain mode.

A young man who had language abilities in both hemispheres was being tested for left-brain and right-brain responses at Cornell Medical School. When asked what career he wanted, the young man's left brain instructed him to say that he wanted to be a draftsman, but when the question was directed to his right hemisphere, his left hand chose Scrabble letters to show that his right brain wanted to be a race-car driver. When each hemisphere has a different goal, it is important to recognize this ambivalence.

By the time you reach the exercises for "Other" Hand Writing you will probably be in a right-brain mode. While in this dream-like state, using your left hand will often put you in touch with your un-conscious needs and goals.

But I want to remind you that the right brain should not always have the final word. Its suggestions may be unwise for reasons best understood by the left hemisphere. But to know what the right brain is feeling about a subject will at least bring about some communication between the two separate minds that exist within your brain.

Category 6.
Sensory Stimulation

Think of a rose, a Beethoven Sonata, a glass of wine, a French perfume, and a down comforter. What do they have in common? Your first thought may have been that each item stimulates the senses. Or perhaps the association you made to these five evocative items was romantic. After all, making love is a right-hemisphere experience and all of the senses are involved and work together for the enrichment of the celebration.

When you imagine that you see the flower, taste the wine, smell the perfume, or touch the downey softness of the comforter, you are stimulating your senses and also triggering responses from the right hemisphere. In this category of exercises, you will learn to isolate each of your five senses and appreciate the unique contribution it makes to the way you experience the world.

The function of the exercises for sensory stimulation is similar to that of transitional objects. Both categories of exercises are used as a means of "transportation," to take you back to powerful experiences of the past.

Swann's Way by Marcel Proust includes one of literature's most beautiful examples of how a taste can recall distant memories. Proust describes being given a cup of tea and little cakes called *petites madeleines*, which he had not tasted in many years:

> No sooner had the warm liquid, and the crumbs with it, touched my palate than a shudder ran through my whole body, and I stopped, intent upon the extraordinary changes that were taking place. An exquisite pleasure had invaded my senses. . . . Whence could it have come to me, this all-powerful joy? I was conscious that it was connected with the taste of tea and cake, but that it infinitely transcended those savours, could not, indeed be of the nature as theirs. . . . And suddenly the memory returns. The taste was that of the little crumb of madeleine which on Sunday mornings at Combray . . . my Aunt Léonie used to give me, dipping it first in her own cup of real or of lime-flower tea. . . . [T]he smell and taste of things remain poised a long time, like souls, ready to remind us, waiting and hoping for their moment, amid the ruins of all the rest; and bear unfaltering, in the tiny and almost impalpable drop of their essence, the vast structure of recollection.

You can use the sensations of taste or sound, touch or smell, or sight to reconstruct events of the past so that you may keep them with you in the present. Their purpose in your life is then up to you: They may provide the catalyst for creative endeavors or help you understand why you are making specific choices in your work or in personal relationships. Again, the fabric on the loom of childhood threads its way through all the actions of our adult lives. This category of exercises will help you see more clearly the colors and textures of your personal uniqueness.

Sensory stimulation can also help you enjoy the world with an enhanced sense of wonder and pleasure. Listen to music with rapt attention, isolating the sound of each instrument before you let it carry you into reverie; walk more slowly through a garden to discern the various scents as you pass. Enjoy the touch of velvet or satin against your skin. Look at a beautiful piece of sculpture and experience with your eyes the patina, the texture, the contours with heightened awareness. Attune your senses to provide you with new awareness of your surroundings; you may be surprised to find how this observation of the here-and-now improves your observations of the people and situations around you.

The senses are not experienced exclusively in the right hemisphere; but the way in which they trigger feelings and memories on the right side of the brain makes them valuable to us in this program. In both a literal and metaphorical sense, when you enhance your sensory experiences a whole new world opens up to you.

Category 7. Fantasy

Society gives contradictory messages to all of us about the value of fantasy and imagination. On one hand, people are praised when their imaginings produce a successful product. But when he doesn't produce a tangible result, a creative person is often accused of having a wild imagination. (And you know the tone of voice that is used for that phrase.)

If a person learns that fantasy only incurs rejection, all desire to function creatively may be destroyed. If the dreamer is discouraged from dreaming, not only that person, but society as a whole, will be the loser.

Creative people of sturdy emotional health and great ego-strength will, of course, find their way in spite of society's disapproval. People of extraordinary vision—those dreamers who reach toward distant stars—have always known the value of letting their imaginations play along the outer edges of reality. Albert Einstein, who had a reputation for being absent-minded, fantasized what it would be like to ride a light beam into space. I wonder how many people thought he was a little daft when he said, "Imagination is more important than knowledge." Einstein claimed he thought in images instead of words, trusted his intuition, and said that he got his best ideas, not in the laboratory, but while he was *shaving*!

Fantasy breaks down the barriers of preconception. In fantasy, we can talk with kings and mystics; we can go backward in time and visit with Mozart or Socrates or ride with Cleopatra on her barge. We can go forward in time to be the first to settle on another planet; we can travel high above the earth and turn the rainbow into a long, gentle slide to bring us back home again. We can visit China without a visa and break all the rules of physics that keep us earthbound—at least, for a moment. But that moment makes all the difference.

In these exercises you will also be able to use fantasy to "try on" the effects of current actions; in an altered state of consciousness, through right-brain techniques, you can go forward in time and be twenty years older, then look and see where the road you have chosen has taken you. Taking an experimental look at tomorrow might make some dramatic changes in your plans today. Fantasy gives us an opportunity to play in untested areas and explore the risks before encountering the reality.

My fantasy exercises sometimes are used in conjunction with the transitional objects exercises to reenter the past. Through fantasy, you can turn failure into success by reconstructing the drama; obviously you cannot change the *reality* of the past, but these exercises will enable you to deal constructively with the *feelings* from those experiences. This new perspective of childhood can knock the cold edge right off the sophistication which keeps our laughter down to a smile and reduces our enthusiasm to caution. Fantasy also allows us to think visually and experientially. After we gain this right-brain way of evaluating the situation, we can present the insights to our left brain for consultation.

Category 8. Dreams

Dreams have fascinated and disturbed people since the beginning of recorded history. These wild, stimulating images, tangled metaphors, and complex scripts are the product of the right hemisphere at work.

The exercises in this category offer several ways to benefit from your dreams at a conscious level. Prepare for these exercises by writing your dreams down. If you have difficulty remembering them, the process of daily recording will help the illusive images to resurface. Several approaches to working with dreams will be suggested and you can experiment with them each day.

Ancient cultures, such as those of the Hebrews and the Greeks, believed that dreams were direct messages from the gods. A man who could interpret the messages was held in high regard. The Bible is full of stories about dreams and their meaning. Alexander the Great plotted his battles according to the interpretation of dreams. The dreams of many other great leaders have influenced the course of history.

In the twentieth century, Freud emphasized the psychological importance of dreams. His assertion that dreams were expressions of sexual feelings shocked and angered a society that preferred to ignore these unacceptable and powerful communications from the unconscious. Carl Jung agreed with Freud that dreams represented a direct correlation between the unconscious and the conscious mind, but he disagreed with many of Freud's interpretations of dream symbols.

Sleep researchers report that dreams occupy about twenty percent of the average person's sleeping time—about ninety minutes of dreaming every night, if you sleep a full eight hours. Rapid eye movements indicate when dreams are occurring (called REM sleep). If people are awakened during this time, they can usually recall their dreams quite vividly.

Psychiatrists consider dreams to be X-rays of the emotions; their images reveal the anxieties, wishes, and fears of patients. Dream journals have become increasingly popular, as many people discover that this nightly communication from the right hemisphere is one of the best means of understanding the inner self.

In the exercises in this category, you will learn how to remember dreams more consistently and how to apply the messages from the unconscious to your present situation. Specific techniques will be presented to enable you to more clearly understand the important role the "dream theater" plays in your life.

Dreams have been called letters from the unconscious. Each day in "The Right-Brain Experience," we will open one of those letters and see if there is something of importance in the message. There may be signals that warn you of trouble ahead and of ways to divert it. There may be letters to tell you the solutions to specific problems, or letters that come from the child of your past who is still feeling the effects of unresolved trauma. We will apply several "translation" devices in opening these letters, for the right brain tends to communicate through various complex codes.

Psychoanalyst James S. Grotstein, M.D., has taught me much

about the mystery of dream interpretation. In his book, *Do I Dare Disturb the Universe*, he writes:

> When I was a second year medical student I had a dream the night before the final examination in pharmacology which I remember across the years as follows: the setting was a bleak piece of moorland in the Scottish Highlands engulfed by a dense fog. A small portion of the fog slowly cleared and an angel appeared surrealistically asking, "Where is James Grotstein?" The voice was solemn and litanical. The fog slowly re-enveloped her form as if she had never existed or spoken. Then, as part of a prearranged pageant, the fog cleared again but now some distance away, at a higher promontory where a rocky crag appeared from the cloud bank revealing another angel who, in response to the first angel's question, answered as follows: "He is aloft, contemplating the dosage of sorrow upon the Earth."

> . . . When I awoke from the dream, I recall having a strange sense of peace to which I owed a debt of gratitude for having done well in the subsequent examination. What most arrested my attention then, however, and, I must say, thereafter until the present day, was what I believed to be the beauty and the poetry of the dream . . .

> It began slowly to dawn on me that my dream was a play, or a small portion of a larger play: a narrative conceived by a cunning playwright; produced by an economic and dramatic producer; directed by a director who had a sense of timing, the uncanny, and the dramatic moment; staged by a scenic designer who could offset the narrative of the dream with a setting that highlighted it to a maximum intensity of feeling; and a casting director who had a flair for the medieval and the romantic nature of theatricality. In particular, I wished to be introduced to the writer.

> It was he who intrigued me the most and yet who frustrated me the most because I admired his script but felt frustrated that I felt so alien to him. . . . The self who wrote that dream was admired, envied, idealized, and unknown to me. So unknown to me was he, as a matter of fact, that he might as well have been somebody else.

Through the exercises in the dreams category, you will learn specific techniques for meeting the writer, the producer, and the director in your dreams. When you learn how to ask them questions and discover how to be receptive to the answers, you will be able to use these right brain messages to your best advantage. After all, each of these characters is a fragment of your creative self. The power is within; the decision whether to communicate with that power is up to you.

Gerald Epstein, M.D., a psychiatrist at Mt. Sinai School of Medicine in New York, reported:

> In treatment, I utilize dreams to help people solve problems of everyday living. I ask individuals to attempt to demand of themselves a dream that will answer a question posed before going to sleep. As the individual lies in bed with eyes closed, he or she imagines a white circle. Inside the circle they "write" the question that they wish the dream to answer, and then demand of themselves a dream to answer the question. Upon awakening, the dream should be written down and then studied to see what answer the dream may have revealed.

In a society far removed from our own Western culture, there is an aboriginal people who have made a dramatic impact upon our understanding of dreams and their uses. Deep in the jungle on the Malay Peninsula live a remarkable people called the Senoi. Violence of any form is rare among them; they are cooperative with their neighbors and show few instances of mental disturbance. They are creative and gentle, unique among aboriginal tribes.

In 1972, anthropologist Kilton Stewart, who is trained in psychoanalysis, wrote about this unusual community which focuses so intensely upon the use of dreams. He described a typical morning, as a Senoi family gathers for breakfast. Everyone, even the youngest child who is barely able to talk, is encouraged to report the dream of the night before. Because children are encouraged to remember, they *do* remember. For example, one child might report a dream of being chased by a tiger (tigers are a very real threat in waking life to Senoi children), and his father would then ask how he reacted. The child might answer that he ran away as fast as he possibly could.

Then the father would instruct the child in the proper Senoi way to deal with a frightening character in a dream. The proper response, the father would tell him, is to confront and conquer the attacker; the tiger could only hurt him if he ran away. If the child still felt unable to win against the beast, his father would advise him to call on "dream friends" to help him.

Confront and conquer danger is the first rule of the Senoi household. The child next learns that the tiger, once conquered, must offer him a gift—something useful to him or to his tribe. It might be a song or a dance or a design for a costume, but it must be a nice gift; and if it isn't nice enough, the child is told to go back and demand a nicer one. Finally, the young dreamer is told that he will have his tiger dream again very soon and that he will then know how to behave. Stewart reports that a given child *will* create his tiger dream again and will, in fact, respond with proper Senoi attitudes.

If a Senoi reports a "falling" dream, he is told that it is a wonderful dream to have. He is counseled that the next time he has a falling dream he must continue falling—but imagine he is flying—and enjoy the feeling until he arrives at his destination, where there will be something there for him to learn. If he finds himself in an unfriendly place, a host of dream friends will help him when he lands.

In his dreams, the young Senoi must learn three things that are vital to his maturity: to confront and conquer danger, to advance toward pleasure, and to achieve a positive outcome. By the time the Senois reach late adolescence, they have very few nightmares. But their dreams are always carefully attended to for personal growth, creative ideas, and suggestions for the tribe.

It will be far more difficult for us to manipulate our dreams than for the child who has grown up in a culture where dreams are held in such high regard. And most of us are unwilling to spend the time and energy that dream-control requires. But in "The Right-Brain Experience" we will use a variation of this technique for some of the exercises. Not in sleep, but in a state of adjusted awareness, you will learn to restructure your dreams. In a deeply relaxed state, you will use fantasy and Senoi principles to recreate the dream and rework the events to an emotionally satisfying conclusion. I don't promise that your nighttime dreams will change as a result of this—though they certainly may—but I do know that you can gain immeasurable benefit from reworking specific dreams to gain understanding and emotional power through the use of these exercises. For instance, in my workshops I have discovered that when people learn to fly in fantasy and in dreams, they experience a sense of freedom and an expanded perception of their options in various types of situations.

There is no more direct path to the unconscious than through the door of dreams. In the next six days, you will be able to walk that path using the specific map offered in this category.

Category 9.
Free Association

Free association refers to a sequence of ideas which seems to come without a logical connection. You have undoubtedly experienced it many times whenever you allowed your mind to spring from one thought to another without conscious direction. It happens when you daydream and is easily stimulated by music or long walks along a deserted beach, a wood-burning fire in a darkened room, or any activity that encourages the left brain to relax and lets your non-linear right hemisphere direct the course of your thoughts.

In this category of exercises, you will learn to use free association as a technique to understand your dreams better. After you record a dream from the night before (preferably done the first thing upon waking) write whatever comes to your mind. Let your thoughts drift anywhere they want to go, like a tumbleweed being tossed in random patterns across the desert floor by unseen forces directing its course.

Your associations to the dream are as important as the dream itself; during this free association process, much of the "decoding" of the dream takes place. Whatever comes to mind after you record the dream will somehow be important in the interpretation of the message sent to you by your unconscious through the symbolic language and cunning disguises in your dream theater.

Free association lets the mind whirl like a ball on the roulette wheel bouncing from one place to another before slipping into a groove. But it is not really as "free" as it seems: We are involved in a rigged game. The unconscious mind determines each movement for reasons of its own and, wherever the ball bounces, there has been some strong magnetic pull from the emotions.

You can do a free association exercise any time of the day or night, but it is most effective early in the morning before you are fully awake. At that time, insights from dreams creep toward the light and often can be captured before they slip again into the dark regions of the unconscious.

Psychoanalysts use free association to help people get in touch with unconscious feelings, not only regarding the contents of dreams, but throughout the analytic process. Stanley J. Leiken, M.D., a psychoanalyst in Los Angeles, talked with me about his use of free association in work with patients. He explained that free association is a technique which helps the patient bring unconscious material into conscious awareness. "It's not that we want to get rid of feelings that emerge during analysis," he said, "but rather, we want to constructively integrate those feelings into the present. Painful memories don't magically disappear during therapy, but they become less destructive when they are accepted and understood."

As you explore the sensitive regions of the mind, you will undoubtedly stumble upon some memory of hurtful times. When you do, try to accept these feelings as part of the very texture of your life. This can help you integrate memories of the past into the reality of the present. Our creative potential evolves, not from pale, idyllic childhoods, but from the pains and joys and exquisite struggles that give us our humanity and our uniqueness.

Category 10.
Gifts From the Right Brain

The multitude of gifts that will come to you through the consistent use of these exercises will be chosen by your generous right brain—your creative, intuitive self. But to find the diamonds among lesser jewels, you will need the logical, analytical powers of your *left* hemisphere.

Remember, it is not the purpose of this book to celebrate the powers of the right hemisphere and ignore essential functions of your logical left brain. Our goal is a well-constructed partnership with each side making contributions according to its aptitude for specific tasks. For this reason it is especially appropriate that the last two exercises of each day offer a direct invitation to the left hemisphere to share in the process that leads to effective changes in your life.

This exercise is primarily evaluative. For example, if you sensed the presence of dragons as you moved into new territory, you will be asked to name them, to try to learn more about them, and to define the role they are currently playing in your life. Dead dragons breathe no fire, so any flame-shooting creatures you met along the path are obviously stalking around in your adult life at some level. And now that they are part of your awareness, they will seem less terrifying.

Your left hemisphere will be called upon to help you evaluate the creatures you encountered along the roads of your unconscious. Working together, both sides of your brain will help you decide how to deal with fears and other anxieties that are now available to your unconscious mind.

You may break some creative blocks during the six days in this program, and a sudden gestalt may lead you to begin a new project or to redirect an old one. Your left brain will then offer valuable contributions and help you decide which ideas should be acted upon and which should be allowed to wait on the sidelines for a time.

Although your left hemisphere will be involved in each exercise at some level, this is the first time you will make a direct appeal for its critical expertise.

Category 11.
Affirmations

How many times have you seen people defeat themselves by negative attitudes? People who say, "I can't," only predict the outcome of their efforts with absolute accuracy. How can anyone rise above a limitation that is self-imposed? The internal judge has the last word: Nothing on earth can alter the sentence unless that verdict is overruled from within.

Two conditions are essential for success: positive *thinking* and positive *feeling*. The first is a product of your analytical self; the second is the product of your emotional self. Trying to succeed with only one of these conditions on your side leaves you functioning with only half of your power.

This category of exercises leads you to discover how to reinforce the positive attitudes of both hemispheres.

You will be offered "affirmations," which are positive thoughts to keep in mind throughout the day; they will help keep you focused on constructive attitudes. This will also help program your left brain to stay in a receptive mode for ideas that lead toward success. Visual imagery will be used to program your right hemisphere, so that at an emotional level, you will be able to experience success as a reality in your mind's eye. By programming both hemispheres to expect a positive outcome, you become receptive to options that will enable you to reach your highest goals.

PART II

SUCCESS STORIES FROM THE RIGHT BRAIN

Introduction

They Can Do It–
So Can You

Several years ago, I began collecting stories about how successful people use right-brain techniques to encourage creative experiences. High achievers tend to be interesting folks and it is fascinating to discover the tools involved in their success.

Writer Thomas Thompson, author of *Serpentine, Celebrity,* and *Blood and Money,* told me that he overcame writer's block by learning how to enter an altered state of consciousness through hypnosis.

Philip J. Koen, Senior Vice President of Getty Synthetic Fuels, claims that his success in business is mostly due to intuition. And long ago he learned to program his dreams to solve difficult engineering problems.

Professor of Architecture Michael Black uses mandalas, self-guided imagery, and meditation prior to beginning the spacial and aesthetic components of his architectural projects. He teaches his students to enter the right-brain mode and visually walk through a building in their imaginations before they begin work.

Architect Hal Fletcher, Jr., who drew the mandalas for Part III of this book, is a former graduate student of Michael Black's; Fletcher reports that the right-brain techniques helped him work much faster and with greater artistic results and less tension during times of tight deadlines.

No matter how varied the fields of the people I talked with, some aspect of right-brain encouragement was used by each of them: astronaut Russell Schweickhart has used meditation on a regular basis for many years; Broadway choreographer Ron Field uses his powers of visualization to "watch" a dance in his mind's eye before he consciously creates the steps; film director Frank Perry has developed an approach to self-hypnosis that helps him relax during times of intense creativity; Suzanne de Passe, president of Motown Productions, claims that intuition and meditation have helped her run the company that produces albums for Stevie Wonder, Diana Ross, and The Jackson Five.

As you read the following in-depth interviews with outstanding achievers in creative fields, be aware of how they use the right-brain techniques that were discussed in the previous chapter. A common thread weaves through each interview, adapting to the personal styles and the diverse professions involved.

Not all of the people in these interviews were aware that they were using right-brain techniques; in fact, many of them were unfamiliar with the studies done on the different functions of each hemisphere of the brain. Even so, they developed creative tools that are striking in their similarity to those suggested in this program.

- Watch the role intuition plays in their work and how they use childhood memories or actual talismans to integrate their inner child into their adult life.

- Notice the various processes that are used to induce an altered mental state that provides a nurturing womb for the growth of creative inspiration.

- See how dreams are used and how fantasies and visual thinking are incorporated into personal techniques.

- Be aware of the similarities that indicate right-brain stimulation and of the diversities that show how each person's uniqueness is applied to the process of creative thinking and feeling.

These insights into how right-brain techniques are used in a variety of situations will be extremely helpful to you when you begin the exercises in Part III.

4

CHARLES SCHULZ, Cartoonist

If you take the Redwood Highway north out of San Francisco in October, you'll find the California hills all thirsty and pale, more beige than golden. In an hour or so you'll come to Santa Rosa. Things move at a slower pace here among the hills and the grape vines; you can sense it as soon as you turn off the freeway.

Cartoonist Charles Schulz, creator of Charlie Brown, Lucy, Snoopy, and all the endearing characters of "Peanuts," suggested we meet at the Redwood Empire Ice Arena, a place he owns and cares about in a paternal sort of way. He was waiting there when I arrived, watching the skaters. We ordered tuna sandwiches from the counter and ate right there.

I liked his direct and unassuming manner and his candid way of speaking in a soft Minnesota voice. I rushed right in with questions, feeling that every moment might be precious, but he turned all the questions around and wanted first to know some things about me. It wasn't easy to get the conversation centered on him—not until he was ready. I had the feeling that he would rather talk to a friend than a stranger and he would just bide his time before deciding which I would be.

No one who knows him calls him Charles or Chuck or Charlie Schulz. He got the name of Sparky when he was a kid and it stuck. We took a slow, easy route into the interview. Later, when we drove to his studio, there was time enough to ask all the questions I had about this bright, insightful man who seems oblivious to his own genius.

He sat at the desk where he draws and showed me the cartoons he was creating for a Sunday strip some weeks in the future. His studio was full of memorabilia—books, photographs of his family, and even an old wooden horse called "Sparky," for whom he was named.

He offered to let me choose a few cartoons to include with the interview; the gesture seems typical of his generosity. I chose these three cartoons which seem to reflect right-brain action:

SCHULZ: I think of myself as a very ordinary person, and I say it sincerely. I'm really not very smart. I don't understand economics, for instance, and I was a terrible math student. I was the worst physics student in the history of Central High School in St. Paul. I'm not a business man. But I do have a knack for coining little phrases. I have a knack for hearing a little phrase and knowing how to take that very obscure phrase and turn it into a funny cartoon. I can draw better than the comic strip appearance gives me credit for because I don't have much room there.

But the main thing is that I think about the strip all the time, almost continually. Not from a business standpoint. But because, as one of my daughters once said, "Dad, you're obsessed." And I think I am obsessed with what I do. It's my whole life—the same way as a person may be a playwright or a violinist or a painter. I'm just kind of obsessed by drawing these funny little pictures. And I think about them all the time. And I have discovered a perfect outlet for all of my thinking. Almost every thought that I have on almost any subject can be played on this instrument on which I perform. My ideas are consistent within the medium in which I work, with my drawing ability, and it all just kind of adds up perfectly. That's my theory of what makes the thing work. If somebody else has a more flattering theory, I'll take it. But that's how I've been able to analyze it.

ZDENEK: However you do it, you somehow manage to capture feelings this whole country can identify with.

SCHULZ: I would like it to be better and I think of ways it could be better. But I think I've learned to be as flexible with this restrictive medium as anyone has been.

ZDENEK: Are there specific things that you do to stimulate ideas?

SCHULZ: Well, there are mechanical ways of doing it. I take a blank

DAYDREAMING?
 NO MAAM, I WASN'T DAYDREAMING...
I WAS JUST CONCEPTUALIZING!

© 1977 United Feature Syndicate, Inc.

 Z
 YES, MAAM? NO, YOUR CLASS ISN'T BORING... I GUESS I WAS JUST SLEEPY...
 I HAVE A SUGGESTION... IF I FALL ASLEEP AGAIN PERHAPS I COULD DO MY TERM PAPER ON WHATEVER IT IS I DREAM...
 SHE ALWAYS HATES MY SUGGESTIONS!

© 1970 United Feature Syndicate, Inc.

 AREN'T THE CLOUDS BEAUTIFUL? THEY LOOK LIKE BIG BALLS OF COTTON...
 I COULD JUST LIE HERE ALL DAY, AND WATCH THEM DRIFT BY...

 IF YOU USE YOUR IMAGINATION, YOU CAN SEE LOTS OF THINGS IN THE CLOUD FORMATIONS... WHAT DO YOU THINK YOU SEE, LINUS?
 WELL, THOSE CLOUDS UP THERE LOOK TO ME LIKE THE MAP OF THE BRITISH HONDURAS ON THE CARIBBEAN...

 THAT CLOUD UP THERE LOOKS A LITTLE LIKE THE PROFILE OF THOMAS EAKINS, THE FAMOUS PAINTER AND SCULPTOR...
 AND THAT GROUP OF CLOUDS OVER THERE GIVES ME THE IMPRESSION OF THE STONING OF STEPHEN... I CAN SEE THE APOSTLE PAUL STANDING THERE TO ONE SIDE...

 UH HUH... THAT'S VERY GOOD... WHAT DO YOU SEE IN THE CLOUDS, CHARLIE BROWN?
 WELL, I WAS GOING TO SAY I SAW A DUCKY AND A HORSIE, BUT I CHANGED MY MIND!

© 1960 United Feature Syndicate, Inc.

piece of paper and just start doodling and sometimes, just from making little scribbles on a scratch pad, you'll come up with a real delightful little drawing; and that's what cartooning is, to be able to draw funny little pictures. And it's not necessarily something that's verbal. Cartooning is still, and always will be, drawing funny, little pictures. If I don't think of something riding along in the car coming to the studio, eventually I'm just going to have to put aside everything, take a blank piece of paper and start drawing. I'll draw Snoopy and I'll throw it away, or Lucy yelling at somebody and I'll throw that away, and all of a sudden, bang, there's something that's funny and that's that. I draw cartoons because this is my life and I like to draw cartoons. The strip is an outlet for every idea that I have.

ZDENEK: I sense with you a feeling of "I *get* to work," not "I *have* to work."

SCHULZ: I don't use the word "work," you know that? It's almost a superstition with me. I never say, "I go to work." I say, "I go to the studio" or "I have to go draw pictures," but I never say work, because I always have the feeling that if I call it work then God is going to take it away from me. That's my spiritual superstition.

ZDENEK: I think God is very slow to take back gifts. But in any case, a sense of play usually makes the work go better. It's very special to have that ability to stay in touch with playfulness, with your inner child.

SCHULZ: My wife says that I remember things from way back better than anyone she's ever known. I remember all the little slights from being three and four years old and all the sufferings and things like that. But I'm able to make them into funny things.

ZDENEK: Well, before you can turn rejection and embarrassment and disappointment into funny moments, you have to feel them the way they really are—the way they really feel when you live them. And then you translate them.

SCHULZ: Oh, yes. And because of the ability to do that, you also suffer a little bit more. You pay for it in different ways. You pay for it by being more of a worrier, or having more anxieties than a person having less imagination—a person who can't make big things out of these little things. Because that's what you're doing in a cartoon: You're taking little tiny worries and making big worries out of them.

ZDENEK: On the best of days, do the ideas come to you in a complete form? Do you see the whole thing at once?

SCHULZ: Oh, yeah, sure. Oh, I can see the whole strip, the whole thing right in front of me, immediately. On the really good days, I'll sit here and think of six or seven ideas in one day.

ZDENEK: Is there anything physical that you do to help the ideas to come?

SCHULZ: The ice arena where you and I had lunch is two blocks away, and a lot of times, if I can't think of anything, I get up and I walk over to the arena and get a cup of coffee and very often before I get over there, or before I get back, I will have thought of something and then I'm all set for the rest of the afternoon.

ZDENEK: I know you like to skate. Do you ever get ideas for the strip while you're skating?

SCHULZ: When I'm partaking in any sport or any activity I'll almost always get some kind of idea. Attending a symphony, playing tennis. I'm always coining little phrases. I don't think funny ideas come in sports that could be described as violent sports, like hockey—the mind is totally absorbed at what it's doing. The funny ideas come from more subdued sports like golf or tennis—not while the action is occurring but while you wait for somebody to serve. I thought of Charlie Brown saying, "When I win, it's better for the game." I've thought of countless ideas at concerts. And I think all of us experience the mesmerizing feeling of watching the conductor as he leads the orchestra and our minds begin to wander. The next thing we know, the symphony is half over and we never heard it. It makes you so mad because here you've been waiting for three months to hear Brahms Second Concerto performed and all of a sudden you realize you've been thinking about something else. And you think, "What a waste of time." But in that thinking, your mind begins to travel from one thing to another and all of a sudden you're inspired by the music—by the emotion—and from that I will get some of my very best ideas.

ZDENEK: Relax the left hemisphere enough and the unconscious ideas begin to surface. I'll bet you daydreamed through some of those math and physics classes, too, didn't you?

SCHULZ: Oh, sure. But, as I recall, we were never really allowed to draw cartoons in school. Especially in grade school. Only in the seventh grade one time, when we began to study modern history and the teacher, for one brief period, let us experiment with drawing political cartoons. I think I was the best in the class. And what I drew, she liked a lot, but much to my great annoyance, she had some other boy go over my drawings and make them heavier. It really bothered me. But outside of that, I don't recall our ever being allowed to draw cartoons. But what a marvellous way it would be to stimulate children—to let them draw something funny. I've always been thankful that I have an outlet for all of my emotions.

ZDENEK: When you're thinking about your childhood and going back into those feelings, do you have any transitional objects—any talisman or tangible things—around you?

SCHULZ: Almost nothing was saved that means anything from my childhood. No drawings. I don't have a single childhood drawing. Everything got thrown away. I lost a lot of things during a fire. I have one drawing from high school that a teacher of mine had mailed to me many years later. I used to think about that drawing all the time—and then I opened up an envelope one day and there it was. I remember a lot of things that were very important to me from the age of nine to thirteen or fourteen. I played a lot by myself. I would have streaks where I would be very much involved with the other kids in the neighborhood—when we had a ball team or played hockey or something like that—but I also had long stretches when I'd come home from school and be all by myself the rest of the afternoon and on into the evening. I played a lot with a box full of marbles. I had about six hundred marbles I accumulated and I would not only shoot them, I would use them as outlines for roads to make a city out of them, and I had a set of tinkertoys which I played with for years but they were kind of annoying because they would always fall apart. You could never get them to stick together. And I had a set of iron soldiers, which I got hours and hours of enjoyment out of and used them in many different ways.

ZDENEK: You use the memory of these things in your work?

SCHULZ: I've used almost all of those things in comic strips at various times. So I've made use out of all these memories in the things I do.

ZDENEK: Are there certain techniques you use to get back to those memories? Any sensory kinds of things?

SCHULZ: Um-hum. Smells bring back memories that are very difficult to pinpoint. I think they do it better than almost anything. But we're almost never aware of it. Colors, I've discovered, will do the same thing. I've had two experiences with colors—one is with a copper color. I would see something that would be a shiny copper color, and I couldn't place it until one day I recalled that I was seven years old and my family lived in Needles, California. All of us kids used to play jacks on the sidewalk outside of the school before the bell rang. I had a new set of jacks that were a nice, bright copper color. Suddenly I remembered, that's what it was. The jacks were copper-colored. Another time I was waiting for my wife to go shopping, sitting in the parking lot, and a purple Porsche came pulling up and suddenly that color meant something to me. I couldn't recall what it was, but with a lot of thinking it came to me. It was the color of a top I had when I was about twelve years old. I use those memories in the strip in some way.

ZDENEK: You're such a visual thinker. I wonder if there's some special way you use that ability to enhance your creativity. Any special techniques for seeing?

SCHULZ: I'm continually observing how the folds fall in your clothing and when you bring your arm up how your hand holds the coffee cup, and how I can see more of one earring than of the other. Sometimes I wish I could just stop doing that, but I'm continually drawing with my eyes. It's almost like sketching. It serves the purpose of sketching because what I see then goes into what I draw.

ZDENEK: Well, that's the right-hemisphere part of yourself that is being used.

SCHULZ: Is it really? I'm on the right track then?

ZDENEK: Oh, I think we might be safe in saying that. Since imagery is such an important part of your life, I wonder if you remember the imagery from your dreams.

SCHULZ: Yes.

ZDENEK: Do you write them down?

SCHULZ: No, I don't write them because they're too depressing.

ZDENEK: Are they always depressing?

SCHULZ: Yeah. I just want to bury them and forget them so I can get on with the day. I've always had a fear of abandonment. When I was small I had a fear that my mother and father would get killed in a car accident when they were off on a fishing trip. I would sit out on the front porch and wait, and I was so glad when the car lights would come around the corner. Later on, as I grew older I always had the fear that eventually, some day, I would wind up as an old man in a little one-room apartment someplace all by himself.

ZDENEK: You must have felt very much alone when you were a child.

SCHULZ: Yes. I've been alone much of my life. The army experience— being alone in a city, not knowing a soul. Nobody wants a GI around. You go into a cafeteria to eat, go to shows by yourself and back to the hotel room. In those days there was no TV; there was nothing to do but read. All alone, you sit on a train, ride across the country all by yourself. There was nobody to talk to, and even if there was you wouldn't know how to do it. At least now I know how to talk to people.

ZDENEK: You have the gift of being able to turn the pain into humor— like with your dreams. You don't *try* to use your dreams but still you do.

SCHULZ: No, I don't try. Unless it inspires something depressing that I can make funny.

ZDENEK: You do use the other side of the coin, then.

SCHULZ: I didn't used to have dreams like that. It's only been in recent years. I have fears of loss, that's all. This seems to bother me so much.

ZDENEK: What kind of loss?

SCHULZ: Well, loss of . . . I'm not quite sure if it's tied in with the children or not. Either my losing them or their losing me, or something—I'm not quite sure. And so the dreams that I'll frequently awaken to are dreams that are depressing, and I will awaken facing the day as if this is the day there's a funeral that I'm going to. Yet there is no funeral. But once I get up and I get into motion, and I come over to the ice arena and I have breakfast—well, then I'm normal again.

ZDENEK: Is that a usual sort of morning? To wake with that sadness?

SCHULZ: Um-hum. Though I've got nothing to be sad about.

ZDENEK: And yet you mention funerals. Do you think much about dying?

SCHULZ: Oh, yes. Yes. Especially since I almost did, last year. I never thought I would, at fifty-eight. I didn't think I'd die until I was seventy-three. And all of a sudden, I'm lying in the hospital and I've got tubes sticking out. I don't think I've ever recovered from the loss of my mother. I was twenty. And she was so ill and suffered so terribly. I used to dread losing my father, but I seem to have accepted that better. I was in my forties and he was sixty-nine. So I suppose all those things are tied together in some way. And I'm having trouble resolving that the children have grown up and are going off, too. I like having them around. Yet they're all off in different directions and I'm glad that they are quite self-sufficient. The worst thing you can do is make your children too dependent on you. They want me to just stop worrying about them and just worry about myself, but I can't do it.

ZDENEK: You're such a sensitive person and you seem to be very intuitive.

SCHULZ: Intuitive?

ZDENEK: I think that you pick up lots of things that are never said—that you sense "between the spaces" in a conversation.

SCHULZ: I never thought that I did. I really honestly never thought that.

ZDENEK: Well, my intuition says you have a great gift for intuition. I think you know when people feel shy or anxious, and you do things to put them at ease. I felt at home with you, right away.

SCHULZ: Well, I'm glad you came all the way up here. You helped the sadness go away.

5

STEVE ALLEN,
Entertainer

The covers of dozens of magazines obscure the walls in the reception room of Meadowlane Productions, which is located on the Valley side of Los Angeles. On every cover is a picture of Steve Allen. The magazines—*Life, Look, Saturday Review, Newsweek* and a myriad of others—date back as far as 1954.

Steve Allen's career stretches like the branches of a banyan tree, sprawling in unexpected directions. Scanning the list of credits on his abbreviated "bio," I saw that he is the only comedian from the Golden Age of Comedy in the 1950's who still appears regularly on television. In his spare time, he has written twenty-five books, more than 4,000 songs, starred on Broadway and in motion pictures, made over forty record albums, has written a play, starred in NBC's *The Steve Allen Comedy Hour*, and has created, written, and hosted the Emmy-award–winning PBS-TV series, *Meeting of the Minds*.

I've known Steve since 1970—maybe a little before—when about a dozen of us at the Bel Air Presbyterian Church worked together on a special committee to explore "creative worship" techniques.

Somehow, in our search for dancers and poets and artists of all sorts, we discovered a bond of common interest that was not only spiritual but concerned this complex and mysterious subject, creativity.

News of family and projects claimed the first half-hour of our meeting and then our conversation turned back a dozen years.

ZDENEK: A long time ago, I heard you talk about dreams and how important they are to you. Is it true that you were asleep when you wrote the song that became your biggest hit?

ALLEN: Yes, it is. I woke up one morning—it must have been in 1954—and it was not the first time in my life that I have created songs in dreams, but it's the first time that I was able to remember one. Now, there may have been a motivation to remember that dream, because I had been given this professional assignment and wanted to do a good job. Or it may simply have been the accident that the song in the dream was a fragment that occurred just before I awakened. Generally, when you say you remember a dream from last night, it's because it somehow got up into consciousness. Maybe you got up to go to the bathroom or get a drink of water or you startled yourself from a scary dream, or whatever, and it's the conscious thinking back that makes you remember.

So, in this case I woke up going, "Walk along the street or . . . la, la, la," and I thought, hey yea, that was pretty good. So I just reached over while I was still waking up and wrote down the few lines I had dreamed and the melody was basically all there.

The song was "This Could Be the Start of Something Big"— and it was my most successful song. So, I pay close attention to my brain in those brief twilight periods when it is drifting off to sleep or awakening. I'm really a dream freak. It's a wonder I haven't written more about it because my interest in the subject is so strong.

No one is entitled to say, "I'm not creative," because the proof to the contrary is dreaming. Everybody dreams, so everybody is not only creative but astoundingly creative. I think the dream is, in a sense, the supreme universal human instance of creativity. I don't mean it's better than Beethoven's Fifth or *Hamlet*, or something. But a dream is like 827 moments of creativity all scotch-taped together. But now, break a dream apart and imagine what you are doing in theatrical terms. You are the producer, you are the director, you are all the actors, which is a hell of a trick— not even Marlon Brando could do that. I mean, he would seem funny playing the women. But you are creating your mother, you are creating your wife, you are creating your girlfriend, you're the guy across the street. You are writing all their dialogue, you're the playwright, you're the lighting director—you're making it all seem kind of lavender as it comes through that window and you're making the wallpaper green. You're the scenic designer. You are the sound man. You are in a sense . . . God. You are doing it all. And boy, that is dazzling!

ZDENEK: What about the other uses for dreams? Are they helpful for other kinds of problem-solving?

ALLEN: Very often as I wake up in the middle of the night, the thing is right there . . . the answer, whatever it is. It's not always earth-shaking—sometimes it's simply where I left the car keys or whatever. Then I wake up and I know where I left them. It's often a matter of something that had been forgotten. The computer just goes to work and delivers the answer nice and neat.

I remember, about twenty-five years ago, reading some of Bertrand Russell, some of his autobiographical collection. He had this technique for problem-solving—he dealt with nothing but pretty high-level, abstract, mathematical, or physical problems. He would do his homework—work himself to a frazzle and then just forget about it and have a good night's sleep. And he said in very many cases upon awakening in the morning the solution was there. No more sweat. No more, "Now let me think, I gotta start working 'cause my mind is fresh." He woke up with the answer and obviously the computer had done its work in his head while he was asleep.

ZDENEK: People can learn to program their dreams for solving specific problems. It's not hard to do; in fact, that's one of the exercises in "The Right Brain Experience." But dreams are good for more than work—do you ever feel playful in your dreams?

ALLEN: Yeah. My dreams are big, MGM, full-color, cast-of-a-thousand, Cecil B. DeMille productions. My typical dream covers five continents, every color of the rainbow, sounds, music, sex, space, flying . . . I do a lot of flying. I'm a great flyer in my dreams.

ZDENEK: It's wonderful, isn't it?

ALLEN: Oh, I'm Superman. Till I was about seven, I thought it was possible that I could actually fly. I realized I couldn't fly right now, I couldn't plan to fly next Tuesday, but I thought that if somehow I could work it out and give it enough time and have a high place to jump off from, I might actually be able to fly.

And later, at the age of thirty-seven or forty-two, or whatever, I realized where that very strong childhood feeling came from. It's from the vividness and the seeming reality of flying dreams. I still have them. Almost all of them are both pleasurable and frightening. I don't have any unnatural fear of heights. I mean, I have the usual degree of fear—everybody's afraid of looking over a tall thing . . . nothing unnatural about that. But sometimes, in a dream, I can be up 800 feet and not worry about it. It's marvellous. But if I fly near a wall or the side of a mountain, then I feel fear about that. But I love the sensation. I'm really just like Superman—just whoosh, take right off.

The dreams are marvellous but I always hated the fact that I require so much sleep. I generally say ten or eleven hours 'cause I feel guilty as the number gets bigger. I can stay in bed for twelve hours with no problem at all. And some people say to me, "Boy, are you lucky, I can't sleep more than six hours a night." And I envy them because that would give me six extra hours of working time.

ZDENEK: It sounds to me like you get quite a bit of work done when you're asleep. Are there any other ways you're aware of your unconscious working for you?

ALLEN: Well, there's a thing that I first noticed about thirty-five years ago. It always happens in the context of my leaving one physical setting for another. Leaving the office to go home. But in probably eighty-five percent of the cases, I'm leaving the house. Or if I'm in a hotel in Cleveland, I'm leaving the hotel. And as I get to the door, or go downstairs, or out into the parking lot, or wherever, suddenly I get a message. It's never in words—it's not like a computer going "beep, beep" with a voice speaking words; but the message-without-words is always very clear. If I could put it into words it would go like this: "You are forgetting something; some object." And at first I used to think, "Well let me see . . ." And then I'd think, "Ah, to hell with it." And that's how I noticed it—by *not* listening to it the first few times. And sure enough my wallet, my briefcase, my scarf, my tape recorder—*something* had been left behind. But at this point, as I say, about thirty-five years ago, I suddenly realized, "Wait a minute, now the last six times this happened, sure enough, it turned out I did lose something."

And now in the last thirty-five years there have been no exceptions. Every single time I get the feeling, I now know it's totally reliable. I'd be an idiot not to pay attention to it.

ZDENEK: I think the explanation for that is pretty obvious. You just have a highly cooperative unconscious. There's no mystery to the process. You've somehow learned to tap a natural resource. And you honor it, which is very important if you want further cooperation from your unconscious.

ALLEN: Yeah, maybe it's because I notice it. Really pay attention to it . . .

ZDENEK: It's like the people who remember dreams and write them down—suddenly they will remember more and more dreams.

ALLEN: Sure.

ZDENEK: And then the material that's communicated to them becomes more and more important in their lives.

ALLEN: Right. I've learned to pay attention because I'm the proverbial absent-minded professor and I forget a lot more objects than I think the average person does.

ZDENEK: Well you probably do because you *do* more than the average person.

ALLEN: Yeah, my brain is usually on eighty-seven different things. I'm constantly going, "Wait a minute, where's my . . . whatever." But some part of my brain always knows and the message always comes in two phases. That's the damnable thing. If it said, "Lost your car keys, dummy!" I'd say, "Oh, thank you." And that would be it. But it's always phase one, "Toot-toot-toot: Something's missing . . . ," and phase two doesn't actually come for maybe twenty minutes or half an hour.

ZDENEK: That's terrific. . . . Now if you could speed up that process you'd have it made!

ALLEN: Yeah, right.

ZDENEK: Another good way to trigger the right hemisphere is through free association. Have you ever consciously worked with that?

ALLEN: Yeah, especially when I was new in the joke business. I would get a yellow legal pad and write down all the words that occurred to me about the slice of society I was dealing with. If it was a cowboy sketch, I would write, "bunkhouse, OK Corral, sagebrush, ornery sidewinder, gunfight, sheriff, posse." Whatever would occur to me. Something about just making a list of about forty-two such words and phrases would suddenly get the wheels clicking in the part of my brain that apparently has some gift for the making of jokes.

Most of my comedy writing comes about very quickly in response to some little silly thought. In fact, I wrote a comedy sketch just before I came into the building about forty minutes ago. I was listening to the radio and somebody used the phrase "star spangled celebration." So for some reason or other my attention centered on the word spangled. Ever since I was a child, words have sounded different to me than I think they do to most people. Certain of us in the joke business are either addicted or gifted, as the case may be, with that way of looking at words. Groucho Marx did that—whatever you said, he would take the word and twist it around and make some silly answer to it. I do that. Anyway, it occurred to me that if something is spangled there must be a verb "to spangle," and of course there is. And I wrote this silly interview sketch about a member of the Spanglers Union: If you want some star spangled on your banner or anywhere, on the wall or the ceiling—whatever—you have to call a professional spangler. He will come in and spangle all these. . . . And then it went from there to: The reporter says, "Well now, if you're a stickler for accuracy . . ." And he says, "No, for that you call the Sticklers Union, and they will come in and stickle for you." It's just playing in a silly way with these verbs. And the reporter says, "Well, I noticed that you're a good family man. I saw you dandling your child . . ." And he says, "For dandling, it's a whole other thing."

ZDENEK: That's wonderful!

ALLEN: I dictated the whole sketch just about as fast as I could speak. There was no pausing, no wondering what the next funny answer would be. I could just hear the whole silly conversation about spangling and dandling and stickling.

ZDENEK: When you're developing a sketch for a whole show, do you tend to work quickly, or do you edit as you go along?

ALLEN: I always work quickly. If I write slower it doesn't get any

better, so I just let it out. At the time I'm writing I don't waste a
damn minute thinking, "Ah, this is no good" or "Is this good
enough?" I just do it. Judging yourself is hanging yourself up,
inhibiting yourself. It's dumb. To hell with that—just write it.
Later you can look at it and throw it away, or fix it.

ZDENEK: It's hard for many people to do that—to put their inner critic
aside long enough to let the associations flow freely. It helps to
feel like a child sometimes—to play with ideas, instead of working
with them. Do you find that memories of childhood feelings are
important to you now?

ALLEN: It seems to me I do rummage around in my childhood. I
remember being utterly dissolved emotionally, literally into sob-
bing tears, when I saw Ingmar Bergman's *Wild Strawberries*. It's
been about twenty-five years since I saw that picture, so all I
remember is this one scene: This old man, maybe seventy-five
years old—it has to do with him being able to do what we've all
fantasized doing—walking back through time. This old man is
walking in some sort of beautiful wooded area, with trees and
sunlight and water. And he suddenly sees, across a little pond or
a lagoon, his parents—when they were young. Now he's seventy-
five, the parents look about thirty-five. And I don't know what it
was about that scene—even now I feel myself choking up thinking about it.

ZDENEK: I can see you're still deeply touched by that.

ALLEN: I didn't realize that the emotion itself would come back. That
obviously reached into some part of my childhood.

ZDENEK: Do you have any things that were important to you when
you were a child? Any talismans or transitional objects, that you've
kept?

ALLEN: I'm trying to rummage around in my memory . . . No. I am,
however, an object saver. I have at home about sixteen hundred
black, three-ring looseleaf notebooks. I'm trying to give them to
a university. They're all about every important issue in the world—
abortion, communism, anti-communism, conservatism, social-
ism, China . . . all materials that I've read and annotated. The
whole world is there in that room in the house. I think there's
something compulsive about my wanting all this information organized and available to me. I want to know and study and learn.

But perhaps one of the reasons for that is that practically nothing was preserved from my childhood. When I was fourteen years old, I didn't give a damn. What did I care about a piece of paper I didn't have from when I was nine years old? But at the age of thirty, my first marriage fell apart and I was trying to make sense of my life. I began to go back and look at it. And one of the first annoying things I discovered was that there was nothing. I had—well everybody has—a few photographs, but I even had damn few of those. None of my school papers were around.

So one of my reactions to that was a very positive, productive reaction. I have four sons and I saved every damn piece of paper that they produced from the time they were babies, and none of them would take a million dollars now for this collection. Their whole life is right there, any time they want to go back and check. I often tell young parents to keep those records and put their children's voices on tape. We're all so beautiful as children . . . God, it's priceless. Everybody has the family photograph thing, but I say even that should be better organized.

ZDENEK: We really need to keep in touch with that inner child. It's a way of healing the past when we rediscover the child and accept it and love it.

ALLEN: You're growing, in some ways, every time you do that—climbing on top of that old self, and getting a little taller or bigger or stronger.

6

RAY BRADBURY,
Writer

Angry black clouds hunkered down over the city as rain threatened Beverly Hills this September afternoon. Sidewalk cafes were abandoned along Rodeo Drive. But as I turned into the Daisy, there, sitting alone among a covey of empty tables and chairs, was Ray Bradbury waiting for his drink and oblivious to the threatening storm.

A profusion of white hair arched his tan face and mischievous blue eyes; he seemed like the kid and the wise man, all in one. There were hugs and then that burst of his rambunctious laughter. We hadn't seen each other since June when we were both on staff at the Santa Barbara Writers Conference. A frenzied waiter tried to rush us inside but Ray sat down again and grinned at the heavens. The eternal optimist wasn't about to be bullied by the bluff of unseasonal showers.

This man, who wrote twenty books, including *The Martian Chronicles, Fahrenheit 451, Dandelion Wine*, and the screenplay for *Moby Dick*, would have a lot to say about the creative process. With some trepidation, I set my tape recorder on the table and prayed that the storm would hold off.

Ray Bradbury has two distinctive traits: a laugh that starts like a rumble and gets happy before it explodes—it's absolutely infectious. And the way he uses "eh?" like an additional communicating device. His "eh" implies "Isn't that so?" "Don't you agree?" or sometimes it means, "Now listen carefully, this is important." It doesn't take long to spot the subtlety of meaning in the various inflection patterns.

ZDENEK: I know about your fascination with trains. You once told me you get some of your best ideas crossing the country, staring out the window. What is it specifically that the train does for you and your creativity?

BRADBURY: It's an immense, unrolling Rorschach test. It's a long strip of paper on two rolls, like the theaters we used to build when we were kids. And you roll it at one end and unroll it at the other, and the strip goes across the little miniature theater you built for yourself. And as the train goes by, in the daytime or especially at night, or at two in the morning or right at sunset, or eight o'clock at night, it goes through all these little towns. And all the people, if it's summertime, are out on their porches; the kids are in the swings or in the streets playing baseball. And you look at all that and it loosens you up. It relaxes you and an immense wave of love for the whole damn race comes over you. Sometimes you weep out of love for these people who are, in a few years, going to be gone.

I remember two years ago coming back from the East and I looked at all these little towns going by . . . nine o'clock at night, ten, twelve, and I kept seeing my house go by, my house go by, my house go by. The house I lived in when I was nine, ten, eleven, twelve in Waukegan. Same damn house in every town. 'Cause as they came West, they brought the architecture with them and they built the house I was born in in every single town across the country. There's an idea for a poem, now, isn't it? Or even a short story; who knows, it could turn into a fantasy. But I wrote a poem saying, I see my house go down the track, down the track, and there I am in the street playing and there I go again. And God made me in duplicates all across the country. So that's beautiful stuff, eh? And it came from the relaxation that comes from travel which stirs up the subconscious.

ZDENEK: Are you aware of the hypnotic quality of the train—the sound you hear, repeating itself in that strong, constant rhythm? Something about that sound seems to free the subconscious. And of course, the hypnotic quality of the ever-changing scene . . .

BRADBURY: Yes, I think so. But the train also stirs up again the things you saw when you were six, twelve, when you were fourteen. Some of the same hills are going by. You are going through the same towns: Gallup hasn't changed one iota in fifty years. Same damn town I went through on the bus when I was twenty-nine and very poor. So I've traveled by Greyhound, by train, by car— and this train thing stirs that up. And it brings back memories of your mother, your father, your brother—all these things that are family. And then, on top of that, you begin to cross-pollinate ideas from your past and it romances you into a certain kind of nostalgia and then the ideas begin to pop to the surface. Like myself going down the track.

And then I noticed the lawns throughout Illinois. And this particular town I went through had no hedges between the lawns of the various people and no walls. And the lawns were a continuous lawn; your lawn is mine, my lawn is yours, so there's a poem there, eh? It's all one big, green pond with the houses in the middle sinking into summer.

ZDENEK: When you get into your childhood feelings, you stir up all kinds of memories. You use those memories a lot in poetry and certainly in *Dandelion Wine*. Is there any other way that you feel that recalling, reliving, re-experiencing that time of your childhood stimulates your creativity?

BRADBURY: Yes. If people will sit down at their typewriters every morning of their lives—eight o'clock or nine or whatever—and begin to word-associate every single morning, it will bring all this stuff up. I started *Dandelion Wine* with a series of word associations. I thought, what were dandelions like? What did they taste like, what did they feel like? Did I make whistles out of them? I did. And you blow them and they only have one note—whereas, when you work on a little hickory whistle or something off the twig of a tree and put holes in it, you turn it into a little piccolo, a little flute. You can play a variety of tunes on it. But a dandelion only strikes one note, just as a soda straw does. On the old-fashioned soda straws, you could press the ends and blow and you struck one note. Of course, the new plastic straws don't work that way. They've eliminated the aesthetics. So you can't make any sound on the new soda straws. But there's an idea for a poem right there.

As soon as you hear yourself say things, you should look back on them and say, "Hey, that's good." Make a note. And so word association begins to build. And you think of your father making wine. You're picking grapes. Your brother, your friends. My grandfather making dandelion wine in the cellar. I wasn't even sure it happened. It was just a thing I felt happened. And I went back to that town two years ago, went back to the town barbershop—which I hadn't been in in forty-five years. And the barber, a man in his seventies, took one look at me in the doorway and threw the scissors and comb on the floor and said, "By God, I've been waiting for you to come through that door for forty-eight years." "Who are you?" I said, and he said, "I was your grandma's boarder in your grandma's boarding house when you were just an ornery little kid!" And he says, "You know the one thing I remember about you? It was you and your brother crossing the street to the field of dandelions, bringing back sacks of these flowers, taking them to the cellar where your grandfather made dandelion wine." I burst into tears and said, "Oh, wow, it really happened!"

ZDENEK: Whether it really happened or whether it happened in fantasy gets all blurred together and at some point is irrelevant, because you build your own childhood to a certain degree. There's just no such thing as remembering how it really was, so you build your own fiction as you go along.

There is a wonderful sense of play in you. Within the man is the little boy, and you're very well integrated with your child. When men lose touch with the boy, I think they become boring men—no matter what they achieve in other terms.

When you get on a roll and your creativity is really flying—with you that seems to be every time I see you!—but when all of your intensity is really going, do you find it difficult to switch back and think of specifics? Such as paying the bills—routine, pragmatic activity? There's something about doing that when you're on a high that seems repugnant.

BRADBURY: Not if I've got my work done for the day. Today I got my work done, so I can be real relaxed with you. But if I hadn't finished it, then I would be a little tenser.

ZDENEK: When you say work done, do you mean a certain amount?

BRADBURY: Whatever it is that feels good. It can be two pages or it can be six—as long as I've done something and I feel I'm ahead of the universe for the day. Every day I have to feel I'm one up.

See, one of the things that we can do is to teach these shortcuts to people. This is where we can really help. We can't teach them to write but we can teach short-cuts to emotion. We can teach 'um how to dig these things out of the deep well, eh? For instance, if you're working on a project that you're too familiar with—like a novel, which takes forever to write, or even a short story that's giving you trouble—you can go write a poem, just off the top of your head, and if it works, even half-way decently, you can borrow the energy from the poem and transfer it over to the novel. You finish the poem and go back to the novel, and you don't look at it.

ZDENEK: Don't look at the poem?

BRADBURY: Don't look at the novel! In other words, when you're working on a novel you should never look at it. I've been working on a murder mystery for years and I've never read the thing, eh! Even a mystery, eh. Every novel you write should remain a mystery; and you should say, I wonder what I did back there? If you remember the emotion, that's what will help you. That's the essence of the thing. These are short cuts that I feel are so valuable for provoking the subconscious to surface again. And when it's bored . . . you've got to watch out for boredom. That's what will kill a thing. You do all these little tricks you can try on yourself to bring the subconscious out of hiding because it's really had it with a subject that's too familiar. Now maybe that's not true for everybody, but if it's true for me, it is for forty or fifty percent of the other writers. If you reread a thing, you're going to kill it! If you read it too often, then you're never going to want to finish the thing.

ZDENEK: What do you do? Finish your first draft and then . . .

BRADBURY: Whatever comes first. I'm working on a screenplay now. I wrote the ending first. I knew where I was going to be at the beginning, then I found out where I wanted to be at the end. And then I wrote a thing in the middle—I'm putting the ham in the sandwich. That works as long as you know where you're going.

ZDENEK: Makes good sense to me.

BRADBURY: So don't worry about a thing. It'll all fit together eventually. Then you can go in with your trowel and smooth it up and fix it up.

ZDENEK: Another thing that accomplishes is to diminish the power of your censor. You can put your censor or critic aside so that everything isn't killed before its born. And if criticism can stay out of the way until all that first flushing gets out on paper—then you can come back and appropriately use the critic later.

BRADBURY: The faster you work the better the truth. You don't have time to make up lies and half-truths. It's like our conversation now. We're having a very fluid shout here, eh? And you're asking me things I've never heard from you before or from anyone else . . . or variations at least. And I have to be alert, instantly responsive to you. If I slow down on you, then you know I'm going to be making up something and it wouldn't be trustworthy, creatively speaking. But if I blurt things out you may disagree with them later. . . .

ZDENEK: You may, too!

BRADBURY: Yeah, that's right! But I respect that. About my early work, people ask, "Are you going to go back and revise?" I say, "No, whoever he was—that young man—when he was twenty or twenty-five, that's the way he felt that year and I'm not about to go back and say, 'Hey, kid, I know it better.' " Because I'm another man here, criticizing. And that's very bad. Very bad.

ZDENEK: It can be devastating to people to start wishing they had done things differently or try to fix something when it's old history. But to love "the child that was" and let him be—with his mistakes and all—well, that seems mighty fine to me.

BRADBURY: You must never compare yourself with your child or with any of the other writers around you. It is very damaging to your creative spirit. You can't be anyone else. You'll make your own little island and people will swim to it sooner or later. You may not have a big audience but just a few people come ashore and say, "Well done, eh?" God, that's gorgeous, just gorgeous.

ZDENEK: But the freedom to be yourself has to come from the freedom to accept yourself as you are in the strengths and the weaknesses.

BRADBURY: Well, I learned early on just how wrong the world could be when it judged my loves. I can't judge your loves. If you're going off into the Himalayas to write poetry, then do it. I'm never going to do it, I'm scared to death of heights! But bravo, eh? When I was nine I collected Buck Rogers and people made fun and I tore them up. A month later I burst into tears and I said to myself what's wrong and the answer was Buck Rogers is gone forever and I was dying on my feet—at the age of nine. So I don't know what kind of thought process I went through—just an emotional purge—when I said, "Hell, I'm going to go back and collect Buck Rogers again. And live again. And I'm not going to listen to people anymore." So from the age of nine I just never listened. I stopped listening to people and their taste. They were always wrong—for me. Right for themselves. But I just went ahead and collected Buck Rogers.

ZDENEK: Do you still have them?

BRADBURY: I have them all! And Tarzan and Prince Valiant and my love of dinosaurs—and because of my love of dinosaurs when I was five, when I was twelve, when I was nineteen, when I was thirty, I got the job of writing *Moby Dick* for the screen. Because that's a great prehistoric beast there. And my love shone through my short stories. John Huston read one of my stories about a dinosaur in love with a lighthouse, and that's how I got the job of writing *Moby Dick*. He recognized the ghost of Melville, even though I'd never read Melville, the ghost that came out of my work there—the ghost of the Bible, the ghost of Mr. Shakespeare that haunted my bones since I read the Bible and Shakespeare and fell in love with the poetry. So it's just living day to day, one passion after another and just trusting all your passions that later accumulate on eighteen different levels. A good example is some-one like the archaeologist Schliemann. Homer spoke to him in his sleep and in his waking hours. And Homer said to Schliemann when he was a boy of ten, eleven, twelve or so: "Troy exists—it really exists—even though everyone else says it doesn't exist. Don't listen to them!" And Schliemann, wise, intuitive boy said, "Hey, I believe blind Homer, I'm not going to listen to you guys. Someday I'm going to get a spade and I'm gonna go dig and I'm going to find Troy. I'll be the one who discovers Troy, three thou-sand years later. And all you dumb bunnies, you get out of the way." And he went when he was fifty-five or sixty, I think, with his wife, and he dug a few miles north of where Homer said to dig and, by God, not only was Troy there, but nine levels of the city of Troy. Nine different kinds of Troy. And when he left, thirty more Troys were discovered. Not only were the doubters wrong, they were wrong thirty-nine times! So there's your metaphor for creativity. There's a Troy in you that needs to be dug up. Don't listen to anyone. Go do it. And if you don't find anything there, at least you can say you dug.

ZDENEK: And there's a great joy in the doing of it.

BRADBURY: Damn right!

ZDENEK: Do you keep any transitional objects around when you work, any particular things from your childhood that stir special memories?

BRADBURY: Oh, yeah. In the basement at home I'm surrounded by books and toys and paintings and maps from the age of three on up. And then in my office—the Smithsonian people stuck their heads in my office four years ago, looked around and said, "You're hired." And I said, "Why?" And they said, "It looks like our basement." So I've got all this junk and I have to tread a path through it. You see, I figured I didn't ever want to have an office, I wanted to have a nest. And it's gotta be packed 'round with the images of all the things I've loved, so I'm totally comfortable in there. A giant nest. I always promise to clean it up someday, but it hasn't been cleaned in years because I've got things on the floor everywhere.

I'll give you an example of another way I work. The people at Bell Telephone came to me about ten years ago and they said, "What do you think of holograms?" (They were starting to come on the scene—laser beams and what have you, three-dimensional photography.) And I said, "I think it's fascinating." And they said, "Well, we would like for you to write a short story for a two-page spread on Bell Telephone about holograms in the future." "Well," I said, "I don't do that sort of thing. I don't take commissions, I don't write ads, I just don't want to do that. And the chances of doing anything good for you are very small." And they said, "Well, tell you what. Carry this stuff around in your briefcase and look at it on occasion. Maybe your subconscious will trigger after awhile." So I said, "Okay"—not believing anything would happen. And about a week later I went to someone's home, and this guy trots out a laser beam and some holograms and I see my first holograms right there in front of my eyes. So you can look around the sides of these vases or statues or airplanes or whatever. Why, I went out of my head it was so beautiful. And I went home to the briefcase, okay? And I did a whole thing about a home of the future where everyone in the house has his or her own holographic ghost in their own rooms. The girl has the ghost of Cathy from *Wuthering Heights* who rises up in the snow and wails outside her window and says, "H-e-a-t-h-c-l-i-f-f." And the boy has the hound of the Baskervilles hidden, and the hound rises up at midnight, howling "o-o-o-o-o-o-o-o-o." The father has Hamlet's father's ghost speaking Shakespeare to him in the library. And mother has a cooking witch in the kitchen who leans over her shoulder and says, "Stir this, do that." So, geeze! The whole thing wrote itself in twenty minutes, eh?

ZDENEK: When there's something you need and it comes to you and you didn't go seeking it, and by golly there it is—these things merge and . . . your story is born.

BRADBURY: Yeah, that's right. That's the other thing to learn too. Never put off. The instant lightning strikes, jump out of your chair and run and go do the poem or the story or the novel. And don't tell anyone. That's another thing, never talk about things. Get it done. Then you'll have something to show people. Then they can criticize the story. But don't tell them the idea because then they'll criticize and kill it dead.

We have this terrible temptation. It's part of our egos to show off and say, "I've got the greatest idea today." No, no, no! *Go write it!* And then take the paper and hand it to somebody and say, "Read this!"

It increases your energy. It's like any love affair. The relationship between sexuality in life and creativity in life is one-to-one as far as I'm concerned. And a great love affair (which means anyone in love with anyone) is the center of your life. If you're really in love with someone you don't want to spread your love around. You and the story are having a love affair and no one must know about it until it's over and finished and you move on to the next love. Then you can hand the first love to people and say, "Hey, this is what happened to me last week. And what do you think of that?" Then you can take the criticism because it's finished.

ZDENEK: What about dreams? Do you ever use them in any way in your work?

BRADBURY: I like that lovely period in the early morning when you're half-in and half-out of sleep and you're in a free-association state. Where a metaphor comes this way, and one comes that way, and they collide and make a new metaphor. And if you have enough energy, you get out of bed quickly and write it down. But that's not the regular dream state. It's the in-between, which to me is the most important. Because it's a relaxed state. And every afternoon since I was a child I take a nap. I never really go to sleep, but my mind is balanced like a feather in-between. Then before I lie down I say to my subconscious, "Now, we have a little problem here, would you help me? And I'm going to lie down now and I'm going to turn my back and pretend you're not even there." And quite often I solve problems and jump up from my nap and run to the typewriter. And everything is answered. So that's a good thing for people to play with.

ZDENEK: Sometimes, through guided imagery, I take people into outer space and I teach them to fly. Do you ever fly in your dreams or fantasies?

BRADBURY: Oh, God yes! That goes way back in all of our lives, doesn't it? It's supposed to be one of the most primitive things in all dream states—for all people, supposedly. Flying dreams, witch dreams, being-pursued dreams. Sometimes you're rooted to the ground and can't escape when people fly at you. Other times you take off and fly and get away. And this seems to be a constant. And that's why we love those fairy tales in which people fly.

ZDENEK: Do you ever use imagery to create special daydreams?

BRADBURY: I do it at the typewriter. The moment I feel something like that coming on, I go right to the typewriter. Flying or going to another place, and getting it onto paper are experienced at the same moment. The two are one for me.

Lying in bed, I've sometimes written part of a poem in my mind. That's always a mistake. You've got to run to the typewriter and get it down 'cause by the time you've imagined the whole poem—at least in my case—I can't remember the lines. So here I am writing all these Alexandrian couplets, and by the time I get up it's all gone. The idea may still be there but not the words, and that's heartbreaking. So, I've learned when the first line comes into my head I get up and write it down.

ZDENEK: Is there anything physical that you do to enhance your creativity?

BRADBURY: I swim. Swimming is wonderful—the total thing of the whole body. And lying in the sun and reading poetry. Then I run back and forth all day from the pool to the typewriter.

ZDENEK: You write poetry with such amazing speed—I saw that when you visited my workshop one day in Santa Barbara. Do you by chance have the poem you wrote there?

BRADBURY: Somewhere.

ZDENEK: Would you let me use it in my book?

BRADBURY: Sure. I'll try and find it. I wonder where it is? All right.

ZDENEK: I kept watching you that day in my class while you were working the exercise. The words seemed to come faster than you could write. I wondered if you *ever* block on anything?

BRADBURY: No, I refuse. And that's a good question, God bless you! I refuse to be intimidated by something that looks like a block. The instant something starts giving you a problem—walk away from it. Treat ideas like cats if they won't behave. Dogs come up and lick you but cats say, "You're not quite good enough for me." So an idea sometimes behaves like a cat. The secret is to walk away from it. Then the cat says, "What was that about? I haven't seen that before. He must know something I don't know." Then the cat follows you. Because you turn like a cat and walk away. You are haughty, too. So treat ideas that way, too, eh? If it's getting you in trouble, don't pay attention to it 'cause it's going to love giving you that problem. And gonna love blocking you. So you say, "Screw it! I'm gonna go do a poem, gonna go do part of a play. I'm gonna go swim."

Another thing that's very important to point out is what intuition can do for us. If we pay attention to it we can stay well. If we listened to our stomachs more often, all of us would have better lives.

I had an idea cooking with a film company. I had always wanted to do this thing but I was afraid they would cut down the budget and all these things they do behind my back. So I went to a final meeting and I looked around at all these grinning faces— but this is long before *Jaws*, right?—and I looked at all these sharks' mouths and barracuda teeth and I said, "Excuse me one minute." I was ready to sign the contract for the whole deal—

hey, it was a million dollars altogether. Then I went back to my office and I called them. I said, "Guess where I am?" They said, "What happened? Where are you?" I said, "I'm back in my office." And they said, "What!" And I said, "The deal's off." And they said, "Why?" And I said, "Because I don't trust you." Hey, Marilee, we're getting wet.

ZDENEK: Yeah, right. But only a little. You really trusted your instincts.

BRADBURY: They've hated me ever since, but what the hell!

7

CLEO BALDON,
Designer

She walks into a room and she owns it. Just like that. With a sense of quiet power, of contained energy, of personal style. Wherever Cleo Baldon stands, that's center stage.

I once knew a cat named Matilda, whose fur was the same tawny color as Cleo's hair. Matilda would watch you from the mantle with mysterious topaz eyes and you were sure she knew a thousand secrets—and all of them about you. I get that same feeling from Cleo.

She showed me through the Galper-Baldon Building on Venice Beach. From this spectacular place, she designs furniture and houses, gardens and spas. The building was once a synagogue, long ago abandoned. Cleo and her partner turned it into an extraordinary working space for their design firm. Think of a high, vaulted ceiling, an old terra cotta floor, indoor trees, a wide catwalk full of offices, drafting tables, something from everywhere covering the walls, a skinny photograph that stretches tall from ceiling to floor, an antique saddlebag strewn over the banister, Oriental rugs. And out the window, a wide stretch of golden sand that almost bumps into the building and, beyond that, the Pacific Ocean sprawling forever to the west.

Wherever you're from, it's nothing like Venice, California. Cleo and I watched the passing parade of locals on the wide sidewalk/boardwalk/strand. Kids on silent skates with their heads wired for sound by Sony Walkmans, old people from distant lands strolling toward nowhere, a doper or two or more, artists and street vendors. "It's quiet today," Cleo said. "You should be here on the weekend."

We spread a huge old blanket on the sand, opened the picnic basket and started the tape recorder, which rolled on and on as it trapped the sound of the sea and that low, faintly-accented voice of Cleo Baldon telling secrets about herself.

ZDENEK: There's a quality about you that makes me feel you're extremely perceptive—that you have unusually strong insights into what people are thinking.

BALDON: Well, as a child, I was what they called psychic. My aunt and I had a telepathic relationship that was beyond understanding. If she knew what was in a package, I knew it too. It was very strong. My aunt was quite amazing. She used to read tea leaves in the back booth of Hinkley's Sweet Shop.

ZDENEK: She must have been quite a character.

BALDON: Oh, she was a witch, there's no question about it. She had cataracts that gave her eyes a glazed look, and when she fastened them on you in order to see you at all, you had the feeling she went way into your head. She worked out of that booth at the sweet shop, and the ladies listened to her advice and took it. They would bring her their marital problems and their job problems and she would advise them, and they would come back and tell her how it worked out.

ZDENEK: Did she have any influence on your creative ability?

BALDON: Enormous. An enormous influence. When my mother died, my cousin came to the funeral. Afterward a friend was going on and on about my mother and what a lovely lady she was—and my cousin was getting more and more restless, and finally she said, "Yes, she was a wonderful woman and a wonderful teacher, and a nice friend and a good aunt, but she was a damn poor mother."

I thought I was the only one in the world who knew she was a damn poor mother. But my grown cousins were all worried about me; so they sent their mother, this aunt, to live with us. And she stayed about three years and performed a lot of things that a mother should, and that meant a lot to my childhood.

ZDENEK: Do you think about your childhood very much?

BALDON: Oh, yes. I think about it a lot. There are things I never solved and I keep going back to them.

ZDENEK: Do you tie those thoughts to parallel events in the present day?

BALDON: Probably. Like seeing something that reminds you of something from years ago. And smells are really nostalgia-makers.

ZDENEK: Smells and sounds too. Music, for instance.

BALDON: And a certain kind of tea will do it. Tea is very personal. I don't know why tea is more personal than coffee. But it is. At least for me.

ZDENEK: To almost all the creative people I've talked with, childhood is very important. Other people, more prosaic perhaps, will say they don't have time for the past; they don't want to look back. But artists, and creative people of all sorts, seem to need to return to their childhood.

BALDON: I hear people say they don't remember things that happened when they were eight and I don't know how that's possible.

ZDENEK: If they created a psychological block to avoid emotional pain, then they wouldn't remember. Sometimes, when I see your work, I feel the influence of the child-Cleo. Like that sofa you designed that was in the window at the Pacific Design Center: it curved and turned and was so whimsical and wonderful that it made me smile every time I saw it. It seemed as if you were playing instead of working when you designed it. As if the child-Cleo created it and then the adult-Cleo made it work.

BALDON: Well, that's something called style. I don't know what style is, but you have to have it. And there's a quality of a woman's style, of knowing what's right for her—sometimes I'll be shopping for five houses I'm doing, and I have these five women in my head, besides me. And things jump off the wall for Mary and something jumps off the wall for Jane. And they're not interchangeable at all. I don't know what that is, but I know when it's right. It's an intuition.

ZDENEK: If a manufacturer calls you and says they need a sofa for the January market, what is your first mental process?

BALDON: I'll get a lot of books or magazines and just start looking at pictures—not even of sofas. I'll look at pictures of luggage, clothes, anything—until I'm saturated with all the goodies in the world and excited about how pretty the world is. And during that process, I'll look at other people's sofas until I hate them, and I'll be very critical of all the sofas that I see and then I'll go very rapidly into a phase which is ushered in by something that says, "All right, so that's terrible; now what can *you* do?" And then I start to sketch; the research is over and my head is turning and I'm sick to my stomach and it's awful and I sketch endlessly. I may sketch for six days and I'll come up with maybe four sofas that I show and they'll buy one. And it's an horrendous process. But it's worth it.

ZDENEK: When you make these sketches, are you criticizing them as you go?

BALDON: No, I'm pretty much sliding free. Scribbling.

ZDENEK: You're not judging as you go along?

BALDON: No. I never judge in the early stages. But sometimes I'll get off on something else; if I have a few days to do something, I'll get off on another idea and sketch that. Then I can get back to what I was doing about the sofa.

ZDENEK: Can you draw from the energy of that other thing you're sketching—that thing that has no pressure associated with it— and bring it back into your work on the sofa?

BALDON: Oh, yes. Yes. Because the demarcation between objects is not that strong with me. Everything is so related.

ZDENEK: Luggage and sofas? Tell me how.

BALDON: Oh, it's very related. Some of my best things have come after I got a new bag. I had a purse once that was a long envelope that folded in the middle. All the soft things were in one half and then the other half folded over it. I used to come into the office and I would drop that bag over the arm of my chair and it felt so good. It just cuddled in next to me and it felt so very good. And I thought, well why don't we just do that with a cushion on each side? So I made up a little mock-up cushion and it felt so nice— that surface softness. Like a mother's lap. The bones are the chair and the cushion is the flesh. It felt wonderful, so I knew I had to design that chair. And I did. Now you see them all over the world. Everybody's done it. That little cushion at the end, folded over. Lots of ideas have come from my own purse. The straps, for instance. And the methods of closure.

ZDENEK:　In Arthur Koestler's book *The Act of Creation*, he talks about "bisociation," making huge leaps of insight to connect unrelated items. That's just what you're doing.

BALDON:　I've always made associations from things that are way, way far afield. One of the things in my landscaping work that is most characteristic is different levels. And I'll always do some dramatic thing—envisioning a party, envisioning how people move in the landscape. I always give them a kind of stage riser to declaim from. The first time I was really aware of that was at a performance of *Hamlet*; I became aware of how exciting the staging was, in the sense of giving the characters a place to superimpose upon each other. It reminded me of painters, such as Rubens and Rembrandt, who placed angels above each other so you could see their faces and I kept thinking of how they painted crowd scenes rising various levels. I was so excited I was up until four in the morning. This had an enormous influence on what I do in staging people's gardens.

ZDENEK:　That's beautiful! It's the same mental process you used to connect the purse and the sofa. I think once you get the knack of looking at the world that way—of plucking flowers from everywhere to make your own bouquet—that ability must infiltrate your total approach to life. I've sensed from the first time I met you that you don't approach problem-solving in the traditional, ordinary ways.

BALDON:　No, I don't. Never head-on. But in the landscaping jobs, when we're going very fast and the deadlines are very close, I can sit and solve the problem by walking on the paper in my mind. Mentally, I become less than one inch high. I have to really get down into it. Like Alice in Wonderland. I just become small enough to move around. And when I get down into it, a line begins to mean something: That line is a pool edge and I'm *there* and I begin to visualize it. Then I look at the various combinations that could work. It's just geometry—starting with a circle and working off from that. And if I'm interrupted I have to come back to regular size and then do my Alice number again.

ZDENEK:　Suppose you were small like Alice, and someone came in your office and asked you a question; can you put words to that process of "coming out"?

BALDON:　Irritating.

ZDENEK: Indeed! Then is it hard to get back down?

BALDON: I have to make a very conscious effort to get back. A cup
of tea helps.

ZDENEK: Do you ever have difficulty getting into that role of becoming
a miniature character in your creation?

BALDON: Oh, yes. Sure. Sometimes I feel great resistance. If I'm not
careful, I'll start sharpening pencils and looking through the mail.
It's best just to make myself do it. I just do it. Sometimes I have
to sit quietly and just be filled with well-being.

ZDENEK: "Filled with well-being" is a wonderful image. I like that.

BALDON: I've never experienced this in words; I don't know if I'm
going to be able to tell you. But I do a certain relaxation thing
through my body, starting with my shoulders down to my stomach
and eventually to my feet, and then I'm relaxed and ready to go
again. I do it when things get crazy.

ZDENEK: Like autogenics or biofeedback training?

BALDON: I don't know those terms. I just do it.

ZDENEK: Sounds like the same sort of thing. You must use other
techniques for imagery, or visualization.

BALDON: Oh, yeah. Sure. In my field the importance of visualization
is enormous. Not only to get a great product, but also to avoid
relying on your liability insurance. You really have to be able to
see how something is going to go together. I have several levels
of visualization. I can sketch something and I know what it's
going to look like. And as I work, I can see it a little better. And
then sometimes I can see it in my mind as though it were a
memory. I did a men's store, and before it was finished, I saw
it—not in a dream state—but in a very relaxed state, I saw it. As
though I had been there and seen it. As though I remembered
it. And now I find that I always do that. I just see things as if in
memory.

ZDENEK: What about those times when it doesn't happen like that—
when the total picture doesn't come as a gestalt?

BALDON: When I'm designing something really tough and I get desperate, I have to say to myself: "Well, you've done it before; you've
felt desperate before. So desperation must be part of the process.
Now let's go on to the next part."

ZDENEK: If you had a problem on a very large job, not a sofa but something like a large landscape job, and you really felt stuck, what would you do?

BALDON: Well, I'd make a very conscious effort to get away from it. You see, I can work until I get so absorbed in my work that I don't rest. But I try to force myself to get away from it for a while. Actually, a large landscape job is so much easier to solve than the little sofa. There are a thousand variables in the landscape but in the sofa, there are only so many things you can do. In relationship to the body, the sofa arm should be nineteen inches high; we know where the average head hits it, and bottoms are pretty much the same, the length to the knee, and so . . . what do you do to be different? That's my scariest thing. When I sit down to do a new sofa I think, "What the hell can you do different than you've ever done before? Than anyone else has ever done?" It's staggering. The chair is the greatest art form that I know about.

ZDENEK: Harder even than a sofa?

BALDON: It's so personal. A chair is very alone. A sofa's a crowd and a chair is a person. It's very personal.

ZDENEK: Can you put words around the things you feel when you start to design a chair? Where would you start?

BALDON: Agony. A cup of tea. Three cups of tea. A walk on the beach. Nervous hysteria.

ZDENEK: Good. You're beginning to sound like a writer. I can identify with that—though it's hard for me to imagine you feeling that way. Then what do you do?

BALDON: I'll look at Chair and I'll start measuring people again. I've measured hundreds of people. You draw around somebody. And then you have to think, well, what if there weren't Chair in the world? What if Chair was wiped out and your assignment is to support a person? So you look at people again. And draw some people and hang some people in the air on a sketch pad and . . . well, it's a terrible process. I'm just finishing one.

ZDENEK: But that's a wonderful experience to go through—even if you don't design furniture. You learn to see with fresh eyes. And there must be a carry-over to other kinds of problem-solving. If you have a problem and you say, "Suppose X never existed, if there was no X in the world, what would you do?" You could apply that to anything.

BALDON: Yes, but Chair is the hardest. I'm concentrating on Stairway now. When I'm in Chair, I can't see anything in the world but Chair. It's the center of everything. Right now, Stairway is all I can see.

ZDENEK: But stairways would be fun wouldn't they? They can be so whimsical.

BALDON: Stair is another of my specialties. We've done a lot of Stairways. Stairway is an adventure. Stairways are crazy personal statements. And there isn't anyone in the world who hasn't made a stairway. When you pull a box over to a bookcase to stand on it, you've made a staircase. Stairways are wonderful and very personal. When Napoleon walked down that horseshoe staircase, he was *looking.* He had his hand on that rail and he was watching, because you cannot walk down stairs without watching. So you're focused.

ZDENEK: Think about all the ancient stairs in Europe and the Middle East and all the worn ruts from footprints, and you have to wonder about all the lives that pressed into that stone and where they went and who they were. A worn staircase is very special. Is there any other technique you use in visualizing?

BALDON: I don't only work in miniatures. Sometimes, like Alice, I get very tall and look down on my work. For instance, I'm working on a landscape project in Santa Barbara and the garden is in ten different places. Some of them are small formal gardens that are not viewed from other places. So I scan it in my head and look at all the vistas. Then sometimes the idea will come fully blown . . . like seeing it in memory. And just now—as I'm thinking about the Santa Barbara garden and telling you about it—I can look out the dining-room window that doesn't exist yet. And I am looking at a garden that doesn't exist. It just came fully into view, just right now, right this minute.

ZDENEK: You saw something just now that you haven't seen in your mind before?

BALDON: Yes. Before now, there wasn't a window. But I saw it completed.

ZDENEK: And will you do it that way?

BALDON: Oh, yes. You might wonder: Did someone else give you that? Or is it from your own mental storehouse?

ZDENEK: Do you really feel like it's the Muse out there, collecting ideas for you and giving those ideas to you in the night, or during picnics at the beach, or whenever?

BALDON: Well, I feel that way sometimes. I feel as though there's this big cloud over us, and we've all got straws and we're poking up into this cloud that has all the current trends and we're drawing it down to us. How's that for a scientific explanation? But how else do people in different parts of the world come up with the same ideas at the same time?

ZDENEK: It sounds sort of like an artist's version of Jung's "collective unconscious." I think those ideas are flying around in your right brain, in your own unconscious. And if you tap that, it *feels* like you've put your straw into the cloud that holds all the good ideas. In any case, I think it's all there. We just have to develop the ability to draw on it.

BALDON: There's another crazy facet to seeing those things and seeing that their time has come. It's called sales.

ZDENEK: Sales? What does that mean?

BALDON: Will it sell?

ZDENEK: Oh, that kind of sales. I was still off in the clouds.

BALDON: I know. You're being metaphysical and I'm being very real. When Chair's time has come, that's when it will happen. You could have given it to a company and they could have stared at it for three years and not bought it, and then suddenly other things happen in the world that are related to it and they *see* it. They pull it out of the file and call and ask for the working drawings. And then by the time it goes to market, the time is right and it's ready to be bought.

ZDENEK: It's that same intuitive sense that enabled some people to make a fortune in real estate a few years ago. I guess it's true of anything—art, books, economics. Cleo, is there anything specific you do when you feel down—or less creative?

BALDON: Well, things have run so well for a long time . . .

ZDENEK: Success does tend to create its own support system.

BALDON: The panic's less. You know you did it before.

ZDENEK: I remember Irwin Shaw saying that when he faces the blank page he breaks out in a sweat. He wonders if he still has it, or if he ever had it, or if he will have it again. It's like da Vinci saying, "When I stand before my canvas, I tremble." Success doesn't take the edge off that.

BALDON: Oh, it's definitely there. Every time I face the blank page. Sometimes I keep putting off what I should get at; and then five minutes after I face it, I know where I'm going and chide myself for the wasted time.

ZDENEK: Maybe it wasn't wasted time. Maybe your unconscious was at work all along.

BALDON: Oh, that's for sure. But the best thing for the unconscious is still just to pour a cup of tea.

8

IB MELCHIOR,
Counter-espionage
Agent/Writer

In the Hollywood Hills, on a knoll towering over Chateau Marmont, Ib Melchior lives with his wife Cleo Baldon and a cat named Matilda.

Ib is the only counter-espionage agent I've ever known, and I remember wondering, when we first met, how that training prepared him differently for later life—differently from those of us who have not had our very lives depending on our wits, wisdom, and intuition.

Ib's work was in Germany during and after World War II, when as a Danish citizen, he volunteered his services to the Allies. He is quick to tell you that the work he did was in the Counter Intelligence Corps of the U.S. Army not the CIA, which did not exist until some time after World War II. His enemies were Nazis and the line of demarcation between good and evil was clearly defined.

Ib has incorporated his war-time experiences into his half-dozen novels (among them are *The Marcus Devise, The Haigerlock Project,* and *The Tombstone Cipher*). In Hollywood he has produced or directed over 500 television shows, a dozen feature films, and several plays. He received the Shakespeare Society of America's "Hamlet Award" for Playwriting in 1982. He also gives sumptuous Danish dinners for his friends.

If you see him from a distance, you'll think of Hemingway, for the resemblance is striking. But closer up you'll notice more tenderness around the eyes. And the Danish accent will convince you that you have not just seen a literary ghost.

At the head of a table of twelve, Ib orchestrated the dinner down to the last note, instructing us in the proper Scandinavian way to toast with *akvavit*. He led Danish drinking songs with a voice that possesses a genetic endowment from his father, the Wagnerian tenor Lauritz Melchior. It was glorious. (After two crystal thimblefuls of *akvavit*, I thought I could sing in Danish, too.)

Later, I had a chance to ask Ib about his work and how he had unknowingly used right-brain techniques as an agent in the Counter Intelligence Corps—and how he uses them now when he writes about those experiences.

ZDENEK: When you were in counter-intelligence work, did you place much importance on the role of intuition?

MELCHIOR: Oh, yes. It's very important. I remember when we had to interrogate people—intuition played a large role in that.

Sometimes we would have to screen people; you wouldn't have more than two minutes to decide whether a person was okay or if he should be interrogated in depth. And after doing this for some time, we developed what we used to call hunches. You'd be talking to a person and suddenly you would know that he was lying to you. It had absolutely nothing to do with what he was saying. It had nothing to do with his papers being wrong. It was simply a feeling that you had. And everybody developed that sensitivity after a while. What you did when you had that feeling was to interrogate the person in depth. And every time I had that hunch, it turned out that the person was lying. Of course, I have no idea how many were lying and I missed it; there's no way of knowing that. But if I sensed that they were lying, they were.

ZDENEK: What kind of people were you interrogating?

MELCHIOR: They were people of high rank in the German army. Party leaders. S.S. of a certain rank. They were people who had belonged to certain organizations. Concentration camp guards. And there were saboteurs and spies. Many of them would take identities that were not their own. And sometimes their papers were forged by the proper authorities. If the police department makes out those papers, there's no way to look at those papers and know that the person in front of you is not the person he's supposed to be. Only the name would be wrong. So how do you detect that?

ZDENEK: You watch their eyes, I suppose.

MELCHIOR: Well, we tried to read people's eyes. There are some micro-movements—little twitches, little things happening in their faces—and we may very well have sensed these without really being consciously aware. It is certainly a possibility.

ZDENEK: I would imagine that even people who are innocent would begin to squirm under scrutiny.

MELCHIOR: It's very difficult for an honest person to lie without something happening in the face. A little artery will start beating or tiny, tiny beads of sweat will show. But this is almost always the case with *anybody* being interrogated—even when you are totally innocent. People always react with nervousness to being interrogated by authorities. I will guarantee you that even though you are perfectly innocent but suddenly find yourself in a KGB office with a couple of scouring Russians asking you questions, you would be terrified.

ZDENEK: Of course.

MELCHIOR: That's the point. Now this is where the hunch, the intuition, comes in. You have to sort out the normal terror, or the normal reaction of nervousness, from the reaction of guilt.

ZDENEK: Are there any other situations you can think of that require that kind of intuition?

MELCHIOR: Well . . . I walked into a village where we knew there was a clandestine radio that had been operating there. It was not operating anymore but we wanted to find out who had been sending out information. We searched many houses and farms and in one farmhouse there was only a woman with a couple of kids. I had a feeling that this was the place, that something was there. We had looked at a lot of houses but this was the only house where I had had that feeling. There was nothing out of the ordinary about the farmhouse. And the woman said nothing to make me suspicious. But I knew this was the house where we would find the radio—and I was right. That's intuition.

ZDENEK: Your right brain picked up the unconscious messages—the infinitesimal hints your conscious mind could never read.

MELCHIOR: I never thought about how it happened.

ZDENEK: No, of course not. You don't have to understand the process to use it effectively.

MELCHIOR: Once we were in Regensburg just after the war. There was a huge estate which had been the seat of the Waffen S.S. organization, and it was common knowledge that its records had been buried on the estate someplace. And those records were of enormous importance to the U.S. Armed Forces. Nobody had been able to find them. Everyone who could have known anything about it was gone, except for one woman who was the caretaker at this estate. And she had refused to say anything. Now you can't make people talk if they have made up their minds not to. You can try, but you can't *make* them tell you anything. So everyone thought it was a lost cause. But one day we interrogated a young girl who was so frightened that she told us as soon as she came in that she knew where something was hidden. She showed us where, in the forest around the estate, a file cabinet was buried. But then she said that the only thing in this buried steel cabinet was loot! Coffee, silk . . . things she and the caretaker had looted and buried.

Well, we still had no idea where to find the records. I was convinced that, in spite of her frequent denials, the estate's caretaker knew where they were buried. So I got about a dozen German prisoners with shovels, spades, and axes, guarded by MP's with submachine guns. And we brought along a Nazi major named Max, who had turned informer, and his dog Rolf. I knocked on the caretaker's door and out comes the woman who sees this whole parade. And I said, "All right, Frau Peukert, this is your last chance. You either tell us where these records are hidden or we will consider you an S.S. member and you will have to take the consequences." Still she insisted she knew nothing. I said, "Okay, you see that dog over there? Rolf was trained by the Gestapo. He can smell out anything that is buried anywhere. Never mind how long it's been buried, he is able to sniff it out. If he finds it before you tell us about it, you will have to take the consequences." Well, you could almost see the wheels turning in her head. It is *impossible* for a dog to do that. She knew that, of course, and she said, "Let him go ahead and try it." So we put Rolf ahead on a leash and all of our prisoners and soldiers came with us. Max gave the order for Rolf to search. And Rolf went down into the forest zig-zagging all around, all around; he keeps going and going and all of a sudden he starts to bark. I said, "Let

him loose!" and Rolf starts digging frantically in the place where
the young girl said the file cabinet was buried. The caretaker
went white as a sheet. So we called the dog back and I said, "All
right, Frau Peukert, we'll give you one more chance. Is there
something buried there?" She said, "Yes, the dog is right!" And
I said, "Fine. Where else are things buried?" And so she showed
us three more places, where we found all the records for the
Waffen S.S. What the caretaker did not know is that the night
before I had taken a large Bavarian sausage on a string and dragged
it through the woods to the place where we knew the file cabinet
full of loot was buried. And I had buried the sausage over the
loot. That's what the dog was after!

ZDENEK: That's wonderful! And a very right-brain approach to problem-solving. That kind of imagination must have gotten you out
of a lot of tight spots. Ib, are there specific techniques you use
that help you solve difficult problems?

MELCHIOR: I'm very much aware of how I solve problems now. And
it's quite possible that I did the same kind of thing then, without
really being conscious of it. When I write myself into a corner,
when I have no idea what to do, I "sleep" on it. If it's a tough
problem I'll take a nap in the middle of the afternoon, but usually
I do this before I go to sleep at night. I'll think of the problem,
and invariably the next day I'll realize I dreamed the entire solution. It's almost as if my unconscious storyteller just works out
the solution to the problem. Sometimes, I won't be able to understand the dream, but the answer will just come right into my
mind as soon as I wake up. Once in a while, if that doesn't happen,
I'll start to work and then the answer will seem perfectly obvious.
I have come to really rely on this process; many times I'll just lie
down on a bed and doze until I get the answer. I keep a pad and
pen next to my bed and at night I'll write on that without opening
my eyes. I think I learned that in the war. When you don't work
from nine to five, when you work all twenty-four hours, you learn
to sleep whenever you can. If you find you have fifteen minutes
before you have to be someplace, you go to sleep just for those
few minutes—sitting up, standing up . . . any way at all. And I
found that during those times my mind was working on the problem and often gave me the solution. Such good ideas came to me
during those times. It's simply the fact that you let your uncon-

scious, or subconscious, do the work. For years I have said that I have a silent partner, and that partner is my unconscious mind. I never thought of it in terms of right brain and left brain.

ZDENEK: Well, no one was thinking that way until very recently. The important thing is to be able to use the creative mode.

MELCHIOR: I'm always calling on my silent partner because my kind of writing, which is mostly about espionage situations, involves not only many people but also a great deal of plot. And sometimes I don't know exactly what I'm going to do in the story. I don't know how to say this without it sounding crazy—but the characters in my books take over and do the writing for me. And as the book progresses, these characters will do things that I had no intention of having them do. And it becomes so strong there's nothing I can do about it. This character takes over, a character that I started out thinking was not very important. Suddenly that character will come to the foreground and say, "Hey, here I am and here's what I'm going to do."

ZDENEK: You begin to feel that the character is using you to tell the story.

MELCHIOR: And this character is the very one that will paint me into the corner—because he will do something that I have not even thought of. And then I wonder . . . what am I going to do? And this is when I go and take a nap and consult my unconscious.

ZDENEK: If your characters always do exactly what you intend for them to do, you're being a manipulative writer.

MELCHIOR: They do take on a life of their own.

ZDENEK: You're a very visual thinker, aren't you?

MELCHIOR: I've always said that my writing is just simply putting down on paper what I see. I can *see* everything. If I write about a man entering a house—I can actually see this man, how he holds a gun. I can see the door and all that's around it and I just write down what I see. Now that's very visual thinking.

ZDENEK: Can you do that any time or do you have to work yourself into a mood for that?

MELCHIOR: It takes a little while. What I usually do when I'm writing is to get submerged in the story and I'm . . . well, I'm half-not-here, if you know what I mean. I will be down with these people and if somebody comes to me and says, "Just one minute, all I want is to ask you just one question, is this red or blue?" And if I have to come back to say, "It's red," it takes me quite some time to get back down where I was before. It's not like a light switch. It takes time.

ZDENEK: When that happens and you have to go back down because you're so anxious to get back to those people you left in a terrifying situation—can you tell me the process you take to get back there?

MELCHIOR: I just simply think down. I don't know how to say it.

ZDENEK: Are you aware of the sensory things going on that help pull you back into it? The smells the characters smell, the sounds they hear?

MELCHIOR: For me it is more visual . . . But, wait. This is interesting, because I do remember writing in one book about a scene where there was a burning theater. And at that point, when I was writing it, I was so aware of the sound of the flames . . . oh, that sounds silly!

ZDENEK: Why is it silly to smell or hear the flames and not silly to see them? It's all part of the same sensory experience.

MELCHIOR: Well, the sound was there; but it wasn't that I confused it with my own house burning down—it's not that kind of real.

ZDENEK: No, it's another kind of real.

MELCHIOR: Yes. It is real in the imagination. We do know the difference.

ZDENEK: If we don't allow ourselves to go all the way in, to experience the sensation, the characters don't breathe. They're just cardboard. We have to feel their anxieties, otherwise it's plastic writing. Do you call upon the child-part of yourself when you write? The little-boy part of the man?

MELCHIOR: I very often draw upon my childhood between eleven and seventeen—experiences, emotions, thoughts I had at that time. It was a time I learned certain lessons and they have imprinted themselves on my mind. Left mind, right mind, I don't know; but they are things by which I have lived my life. Case in point: Danish education is very strict and on this particular occasion we were told we had twenty minutes for a test. Then the history teacher went up to the back of the class and all of a sudden he started crowing like a cock. He flapped his arms like wings, and then he made noises like a horse and a cow. He put on a fantastic performance. At first everyone turned around to watch him. Then some of us began trying to do the test, or as much as we could; and all of a sudden he looked at his watch and said, "Okay, twenty minutes is up." And he collected all the papers. He said, "The one important thing I want to teach you is this: If you have something important to do, let *nothing* distract you." I've never forgotten it. And I hear his cock-a-doodle to this day, if I start getting distracted.

And then there is a story that became an enormous part of my life. It was the first story I read when I was learning Swedish. The moral of the story was that there is always a third way out. You are never in an "either/or" position. You must not think, "I have to do this or I have to do that"—there is always the third way out. The story is of a little boy on a sled pulled by a horse. He has a big cask—a barrel—on the back of his sled and the wolves are coming. He thinks he is faced with doing one of two things: Either he can try to make it home ahead of the wolves, which he knows he cannot do, or he has to stop and fight the wolves, and he knows he cannot do that, either. So he looks for the third way out. He turns the horse loose, knowing it will run for the barn and alert his father, and he turns the cask upside down and hides inside of it. That third way out, of course, saved his life.

I have many times remembered that story and reminded myself to find the third way out.

ZDENEK: I'll bet that kind of thinking is imperative for counter-intelligence work. Have you ever done any mind-over-body techniques when you're under a lot of pressure?

MELCHIOR: Well, I have learned to bring my heartbeat to exactly what I want it to be. My doctor said I have to bring my heartbeat down to between sixty-two and sixty-four—ten beats slower than it used to be. Of course there are medications that I could have taken, but I don't like medications. So I learned to slow down my heartbeat and for years I have been able to keep it down. If it starts to go faster, I start counting; and I count slower and slower, and in a very little while it will be right where I want it to be.

ZDENEK: Did you have biofeedback training to learn to do that?

MELCHIOR: No, I just taught myself. The mind can do anything. Once, in the war, I knew that some important Nazi papers were hidden in a house on the Moselle River in a little town in Luxembourg. The Moselle is not a very large river and the Germans were on the other side. I had to get to this house by moving along the river on a street that was under enemy observation. The German troops were directly across the river and were watching for anyone moving on the street. Now, I had never been shot at before: In battle it's always the other guy they're shooting at, not you. Nobody had ever actually looked at me and said, "We're going to get this guy." But this time I was alone and their shooting was very much aimed at me. What can you do when people are shooting at you and you know you have to keep going? I started running as a machine gun opened up, and I knew I had to keep going. I couldn't think about being hit—I remember thinking of the interesting sounds the bullets were making as I ran past a wall. The sounds were different on the different kinds of walls. How can the mind do this? How can it focus on some other thing so that you can do what you have to do without terror?

ZDENEK: I don't know. But the mind has many powers we are only beginning to discover. By the way, did you get the plans you were after? Were they in the house by the river?

MELCHIOR: Oh, I got them all right—thanks to the help of my right brain, or my left brain, or both!

9

ROBERT McKIM, Professor, Stanford University

If you wander the spacious grounds of Stanford University long enough—as I did one crisp November noon—you will eventually find the Terman Engineering Building and, on the fifth floor, the office of Professor Robert McKim. He doesn't like to be called professor, though; he takes a negative view of labels that separate people. Robert McKim is unlike any of the professors I've ever known. For one thing, he's as good a listener as a talker—and when he talks, you want to hear more.

McKim teaches serious and ambitious students to rediscover the value of fantasy and imagination—and many other good things they were encouraged to lay aside as they were growing up. If you were one of the lucky Stanford students accepted for McKim's class in Visual Thinking, this is what you would encounter:

After attending several classes to learn relaxation techniques, you enter the "Imaginarium"—an extraordinary place where you discover radically different ways of observing your world and yourself. You lie inside this geodesic dome with as many as fifteen others, your bodies arranged like the spokes of a wheel, your heads on a huge common pillow. Many kinds of experiences await you—and for each of you the experience will be different.

After viewing the Imaginarium, which was McKim's invention, we returned to his office, which overlooked a reflection pool and the carefully landscaped garden of the university. He leaned back in his chair, and spoke of the Imaginarium with pride and no small amount of excitement.

ZDENEK: What happens as soon as people are settled into the dome?

McKIM: You start by learning how to relax. You lie down in the geodesic dome and listen to a professional announcer and sound
effects, and you're allowed to go into a deeply relaxed state. It's
almost like hypnotic induction; it's just very deep relaxation. Then
we show you the power of imagination to move in space and time.
By watching pictures projected onto the ceiling of the dome, you
see a boy in a boat on a lake, in the United States, on the earth,
and the moon goes by. Well, if you're lying flat on your back on
this platform with your visual field completely taken up—there's
no frame to it—it feels like you're moving—like you're moving
through space. Especially as you get out to the Milky Way and
then the thing starts tumbling back toward earth again. It's a
demonstration of the power of the imagination to go anywhere in
space—which you can do in your mind. You feel like you're actually doing it. Obviously, the platform is not moving. But it shows
the power of the imagination to create very strong, powerful,
realistic experiences.

We ask the students to visualize an apple in their minds,
and many people have trouble even doing that. Then we show
slides of apples from various angles and they get a more immediate
sensory input about apples. And we ask them to imagine an apple
again. Then we stop and give them apples. And they eat apples
and they're asked to have a complete sensory experience of the
apple. Hear it crunch, snap. How does it smell and taste? And
then they are taken on a fantasy where the apple they have just
eaten is becoming them and they become the apple. So now they
are apples on the trees. They hear a dog barking in the distance.
We put the fragrance of apple blossoms into the dome, and they
regress in time. The apple is becoming smaller and turns into an
apple blossom, and they imagine that they become the tree itself,
the sap, down into the trunk, into the earth and the lights go dark
and they evaporate and go into the clouds. And there are sound
effects: Thunder begins to roll and it rains, and they come down
into the earth again and back into the tree. It's a kind of guided
fantasy built on the apple. And it has embedded in it the notion
that you can merge with the image. Be the image. You can see
an apple and you can be an apple.

In another Imaginarium program, students look at the earth

from a distance—from one of those astronaut shots. You can see Africa down there in the distance, and on the sound system drums are playing and we go down to Africa in imagination and visit that African tribe, and you can see the drummer in your imagination. And then we ask them to be the drummer. At that point vibrator coils on the platform are turned on, which vibrate the platform with the vibration of the drum. Then they imagine that they *are* the drummer and we simply continue along lines like that . . .

We're showing them the power of using fantasy. It's not like memory—not just going to some known time or some known place. We start with a very direct, guided program and then we get them to start doing self-guided stuff. After they've been shown the power of their imaginations, eventually they don't need the Imaginarium at all. Well, it's an awful lot to do in four hours— but that's what they can do in the Imaginarium.

ZDENEK: Have you done follow-up studies to see what happens to people after they've experienced the Imaginarium?

McKIM: Yes, I have—though I'm not a psychologist. I've used questionnaires, but these are only subjective reports. It's a dramatic experience for some people; they become so aware of things that are going on within them already. Suddenly they're creating imagery and it's very important to them. Now, in a way, the Imaginarium didn't start that. They had it all the time, didn't they?

ZDENEK: You just put them in touch with what was already there.

McKIM: That's right. And it gives people permission. People don't feel that they have permission to have that kind of experience. Their parents have told them not to do that. There's no reward for it in this society.

ZDENEK: They probably got into trouble for doing that in school at one time or another.

McKIM: That's right. That's one of the reasons we built the Imaginarium—so we could create a setting that would be nothing like a classroom. We give them permission to have a kind of experience that leads them to a much richer mental life—to allow their creativity to be part of that.

ZDENEK: Did any of your students report that they approach problem-solving differently after this experience?

McKIM: Yes. And of course there are so many things going on in my
    Visual Thinking course that everything is working together to
    help them do that. So, some of the results are perhaps not so
    much from the Imaginarium as from experiences they have in
    the class on Visual Thinking.

        Stanford students are chosen for their verbal and mathe-
    matical aptitude, and so most of them have suppressed this whole
    side. But they are very bright and when you do light the light for
    them, there's a significant change. Years afterward, they come
    back and say what a switch that was—it was an important thing
    that happened. And, by now, Visual Thinking is a course with a
    big reputation; only about half the people who want to take the
    course can take it. We just don't have the manpower and the
    space.

ZDENEK: Do you find resistance among some of the faculty who just
    don't understand this type of learning experience?

McKIM: Well, there was a lot of resistance when we started out. But
    now they're so used to it that they've written about is in *The
    Stanford Engineer* right along with the more technical articles.
    The Dean brings his guests up to show them the place and people
    who are raising money for Stanford are brought over to have the
    Imaginarium experience. It is something that's very well inte-
    grated into the University.

ZDENEK: What was it that motivated you to design the Imaginarium
    and the Visual Thinking course?

McKIM: Just a strange series of events. I was interested in teaching
    my design students to make quick sketches. I was interested in
    this thing called the "idea sketch." I realized that my Stanford
    crowd was—well, they couldn't draw. They were just terribly
    illiterate that way. So I started teaching them to draw. I began to
    realize that they couldn't *see*. Although their vision was 20/20,
    they couldn't see the most basic errors in the way they were
    perceiving the world. They couldn't see proportions well, they
    couldn't see fundamental perspective effects, and they couldn't
    tell that they were getting them wrong—not a little bit wrong,
    but radically wrong. So I became interested in drawing and seeing
    and the relationship between the two. And how drawing can

invigorate seeing. I wanted to try to facilitate the so-called "insight" phase of creativity.

We often take people up to the top of the mountain and give them a good look, but they don't know how to get back up again. And so what we're doing now is teaching them how to get there again. We're teaching them to relax in a different way and they learn how to get to the mountain-top by themselves. But a lot of people don't even know what's there.

ZDENEK: There's just no language for how you get there and so it's hard to explain, even to yourself.

McKIM: That's right. There's no map for it at all. Until you've learned to train yourself to get there by sign posts that are non-verbal, it's hard to go back into the forest and find the special place. And to have full access to your imagination, you have to be willing to encounter some of the negative things that might be there. Otherwise, you wall those up—you create limits to how much you have access to. If you go through that experience of confronting the negative, on the other side is the positive.

ZDENEK: Are you convinced of that?

McKIM: I'm convinced that full access is totally positive. There's a psychiatrist at Stanford and he has full-sized ventriloquist dummies that he operates with children and gets the children to relate to the ventriloquist dummies and say things that they would not say to real people. And he says that the problem we're having with the contemporary generation is that they are so pleasure-oriented that when they encounter imaginative blocks—or pain—they won't go there. This cuts them off from a tremendous amount of their imagination. They need to understand that the happy ending is on the other side of the block. But, of course, that kind of thing is too individual to deal with in my course.

ZDENEK: When you are just beginning to help people experience visual thinking, do you ever suggest they use a mandala?

McKIM: Oh, yes. I have a good mandala painting that's quite beautiful. Mandalas can be very helpful.

ZDENEK: Do you use autogenic training or any of the relaxation techniques that are used in biofeedback?

MCKIM: Well, I would consider those to be very close to what we do.

ZDENEK: For architecture and engineering and art, it's easy to see a
    very definite benefit for visual thinking. For people who are not
    in graphic work like that, do you think that thinking visually is
    equally valid and applicable?

MCKIM: I'm convinced that this kind of thinking applies to everything.
    I've had Ph.D. candidates in economics trying to do everything
    they're doing in economics visually. That was the challenge. That's
    why they came into my class. And they can visualize everything
    in any activity. All fields could be taught with visual thinking, at
    least part of the time. In all sorts of classes, this is useful. Grammar
    can be visualized. Math can be visualized. There are visualizations
    for everything.

    And there is a metaphysical issue here. Julian Jaynes sug-
    gests that in the right hemisphere of the brain the voice of God
    is heard. This is the channel to God's commands. If there's any
    spiritual domain, it must be on the right side.

ZDENEK: In recent research they found that people with damaged left
    hemispheres will still have some form of prayer activity from the
    right side.

MCKIM: So you're dealing with spiritual issues when you're dealing
    with the right brain. Actually, it's a spiritual training. And even-
    tually what you're trying to achieve, is a union with—well, what-
    ever it is—whatever name you want to give it.

ZDENEK: Bob, do you use any physical objects as triggers to generate
    memories of childhood with your students? Any talismans or tran-
    sitional objects that bring childhood into the conscious aware-
    ness?

MCKIM: The answer is yes, although we do it somewhat differently.
    We get the students to return to a childish state. What we're
    doing is taking these serious people who are paying all this tuition
    to come to Stanford and we're telling them that they can be
    children again.

ZDENEK: Do you get resistance to that?

MCKIM: No. They come because they really want to play. There's a
    tremendous amount of energy released by the games we play,
    and we've done this for so long that there's already this message

out there that this is okay. In our class we have many projects which are intended to help people return to childhood. We have them draw pictures of their childhood home, things like that.

ZDENEK: Do you have any objects from your childhood that are really special to you?

McKIM: Yes, I have things I had when I was a child—a teddy bear and things like that.

ZDENEK: Where do you keep them?

McKIM: In my office at home. I have my teddy bear and a picture of my grammar-school class. I never thought of it in that way, but that must be why I kept them. There's a large child in me that likes to play. I have things that my father had when he was a child, too. And I have pictures in my office of him as a child.

ZDENEK: What do you think that does for you, keeping those things so visible in your life?

McKIM: Well, I hadn't thought of it. But maybe I've unconsciously been using those to regress to childhood—that's interesting, I'd never realized what all that stuff was about. The teddy bear is missing right now; I think my son may have borrowed it.

ZDENEK: How old is your son?

McKIM: Twenty-one.

ZDENEK: It would be interesting to know how he's using it. Maybe he uses it in the same way you use that photograph of your dad.

McKIM: Well, I get a tremendous kick out of that picture. It is a sort of sepia-toned thing. In those days they dressed him in little soldiers' uniforms. I also have a picture of me, with a toy airplane . . .

ZDENEK: These tangible things help you go back into that time and to recall those feelings. You're keeping the child alive and giving him a special place in your adult space.

McKIM: It's interesting that I can bring that sort of thing out in my classes, and at the same time, not know that I was doing that for myself. I didn't realize those things were out there for that purpose. But it does sound very purposeful, now that you mention it.

ZDENEK: Do you yourself work with dreams at all?

McKIM: Yes, but my problem is that if I get very interested in my dream world, I stay awake a lot. I'll remember all my dreams and make sketches of them and I'll remember them vividly for a long time; but for me it becomes too much of a project and I don't get enough sleep. But I will use my dreams to have insights with.

ZDENEK: How do you do that?

McKIM: By simply delivering the issue to my dreaming consciousness and ask that a solution be given to me in my dreams.

ZDENEK: Does that really work for you?

McKIM: Well, mostly it doesn't, but it works often enough to keep me interested in it. Sometimes it works very well. I get the answer in metaphors.

ZDENEK: You feel the solutions are sorted out in your sleep?

McKIM: Somehow it all gets sorted out in my sleep. I know that most of my good thinking is not available to my conscious mind. So I just deliver the problem over to that part of me that does the good stuff.

ZDENEK: When you validate the process by acknowledging the power of the unconscious, the right brain is much more willing to co-operate.

McKIM: I agree. You have to validate it. I'm thinking about those people in Malaysia, the Senoi. They really honor that side of themselves and it has a tremendous amount of influence in their lives. And I think that when I do a dream notebook, I'm honoring the importance of dreams. It's as if the unconscious says, "Oh, you're interested? Good, now we can play." Now, if only I had more of a Senoi lifestyle!

ZDENEK: Chances of that happening at Stanford are pretty remote, I'd say.

McKIM: Sometimes I think it would be great to be in another tribe, where time was allotted to do these things. *This* tribe . . . does not do that, however.

ZDENEK: Bob, some people think laughter encourages a good environment for creativity. Has that been your experience?

McKIM: Well, it helps the censorship to be lifted. When I'm in a good state, it's easy for me to laugh, to be playful. When I'm stuck in my perceptual rut, it's not very funny. For example, when we start off the school year there are usually three or four graduate students in here, kicking off ideas for projects. When it's all going well, there's a lot of laughter. Laughter's a sign of things going well. There is something magical about it. If I do too much writing that is left brain—with words rather than with images—then my body starts acting up. There are muscle groups that tighten up and I don't feel good.

ZDENEK: Is there anything you do when that starts happening?

McKIM: Well, I used to just keep on writing in spite of that. I no longer will do that to my body.

ZDENEK: That's when you need to do those relaxation techniques.

McKIM: I find that there are places to go in the mind, beyond images, beyond words. Where the sensation is very blissful. And euphoric.

ZDENEK: How long do you stay there?

McKIM: Well, I was actually able to stay there for several months one time. I was able to have that state whenever I wanted to, no matter what I was doing. Then the old habits settled in and I lost the capacity to stay in that state as much as I would like to.

ZDENEK: Was your work more creative when you were in that state?

McKIM: Oh, yeah. It was effortless. Really effortless. I would like to cultivate that again. But it takes time—and it's very hard to work that in with a Stanford schedule. All the chasing around, the committee meetings. You tend to go into a sort of automatic consciousness, which is a lot less than what I was describing. The daily routine sort of did me in. Relaxation is only part of the way to that state of consciousness.

ZDENEK: Can you use right-brain techniques to control your physical condition—such as experiencing the room as ten degrees warmer or cooler?

McKIM: To some extent I can. I was in a group, one time, learning how temperature of the hands could be raised by using the mind. There were people around me who could immediately raise their temperature fourteen degrees. Their hands would actually flush. I could get mine up five or six degrees. I've learned to handle pain the same way. I use it when I go to the dentist. I don't need novocaine or anything. I look at it as something not to be afraid of. I consider it an interesting experience. Learning how differently I can look at it from when I was a kid. That's just another experiment with consciousness.

ZDENEK: I think experimenting with consciousness is the most exciting of the new frontiers. If we can't change the problem, we can at least change our response to the problem. Harnessing the power—that's what it's all about.

10

BARBARA GOLDSMITH, Writer

A cold winter wind rolled off the sea and across the long stretch of sand in East Hampton on New York's Long Island. I turned up the collar of the goose-down coat I borrowed from Barbara Goldsmith and thought how different the mood of the East Coast seemed from my own Southern California home.

We walked for miles that day talking of poets and painters and the nightingale's tongue. Grand old houses lay way back from the sea, pockmarked from years of weathering. They were deserted now for the winter, like huge nests of migratory creatures who would return come summer. But now it was February, with no hint of spring.

Barbara talked about the screenplay she was working on, the books finished and others not yet begun. Gifted, fragile, vulnerable, curious, strong. Five-eight and willow-built. Long hair, thick and rich-brown. A smile somehow both confident and shy.

When we came off the beach and sat drinking cappuccino at her kitchen table, I thought back over the long list of credits she has earned as a writer. Years before I met Barbara, I had admired her first novel, *The Straw Man*. And there was the fine work she did on *Little Gloria, Happy at Last*, which was not only a story about "The Matter of Vanderbilt," but a sociological study of America in its most opulent and devastating times. Before writing books, Barbara was an award-winning journalist, a senior editor at *Harper's Bazaar*, and a founding editor of *New York* magazine.

She is also fascinated by the creative process and is very much in touch with how it works in her life.

ZDENEK: Many people assume that if a person is writing social history or other forms of non-fiction, the person's left hemisphere of the brain would be most dominant. But having read *Little Gloria, Happy at Last*, I would assume that many right-hemisphere functions were involved in that process. For example, did your intuition play a large part in the development of that book?

GOLDSMITH: Absolutely. I rely on it not only when I interview people but even if I'm doing research from a book. Well, let me give you an example: In *Little Gloria, Happy at Last*, I knew that Gloria Vanderbilt's mother loved nothing better than to be in a nightclub every night. She loved the high life, she loved jewels, loved furs—she took, for the winter, a deserted house totally removed from London. And she said that she had done it for her child's health. Now, she *never* had paid any attention to this child. And I thought, "Wait a minute, this doesn't make sense: It's not in keeping with the character of the person." Eventually I found out she had taken that house because it was only a mile to Fort Belvedere, which was the country home of the Prince of Wales. He was having a secret affair with her identical-twin sister, Thelma, and this provided a haven for them. So I discovered something nobody else did. I don't know if you would call that intuition or common sense. But if people are not behaving in a way that is consistent with their characters, then you have to investigate.

ZDENEK: When you investigate, you frequently interview a lot of people. How does intuition work for you there?

GOLDSMITH: I could almost give a course in how to give an interview. Very often interviewers go in and they will not stop asking their questions. So they miss the great trip down the river, because they're going off into these little tributaries which really don't interest the person being interviewed. I think you have to research someone as much as you can, and then you have to listen—that's where intuition comes in. You have to watch for the nuance, watch for the thing that is unsaid—and wonder why it's unsaid. And you have to just roll with whatever it is the person wants to communicate. People sometimes forget that interviews are communication between two people. I find it remarkable what people will tell you if you're truly interested in listening.

And because I do social history, I find I'm in the position to have to interview a lot of old people. You cannot direct an interview with an older person. You just have to have a lot of patience, because they will not respond and give you that nugget of gold unless you take the trip with them. You have to be the way they want you to be or else they won't give you that nugget. And that really teaches you a lot of patience.

ZDENEK: That's fine so long as they'll give you enough time.

GOLDSMITH: Well, older people will give you endless amounts of time, because unfortunately very few people want their time.

ZDENEK: When you talked with people, particularly for the *Little Gloria* book, you were asking them to remember back to situations that happened a long time ago—and to remember feelings from a long time ago. And because you are incredibly observant, you also wanted to know all kinds of physical details. What were the colors? The textures? And the moods? The ambiance is critical to your kind of writing, and yet you had to get this information from another person. Many non-fiction writers never weave a sense of place and mood into their books, but you had it in *Little Gloria*. How did you extract that kind of information?

GOLDSMITH: Well, first of all you have to love it. The writers that I admire the most are writers like Marcel Proust, who create a world through a myriad of detail. And you have to really care whether the blouse they were wearing was red and whether the jabot was ruffled. You just have to love it. You look at all the photographs or sketches about them—if they exist—and you read about the period. Then you can go to someone and say, "Look, I'm told that when women wore diamond bracelets way up their arms that those were called 'service stripes.' Do you remember when women did that?" And very often a person will say, "Do I remember! I have, from my grandmother, this platinum bracelet and . . ." And they will suddenly be projected into the past. Very often an object is a wonderful way to draw out reminiscences.

Or they might correct you and say your information is in-correct. And that's wonderful because they have a whole different thing to tell you. So either way, you win. But for every pertinent detail you get fifty thousand details that don't mean anything. And there is something magical about a pertinent detail—about the fact that Gertrude Vanderbilt Whitney's dresses were so heavy with jewels that she couldn't hang them in the closet and instead had to lay them on twelve-foot shelves. That's kind of a magical detail. But if you say she had a hundred and forty-two ball gowns, that's not such a magical detail.

ZDENEK: But the ability to recognize it when it comes—to spot the gold nuggets—is part of your gift.

GOLDSMITH: And that's all very right-brain. I have only one rule about that: If it excites me, it'll excite someone else. If it hits that little tinkle bell in my head, then that's all I need. It's not intellectual at all. Of course you can also see these nuggets because you are totally an outsider all the time. I would say all good journalists and most good authors are outsiders. They all have their noses pressed to the window. And they don't feel part of any group. So each situation is judged individually and observed individually.

ZDENEK: Do you think, with most artists, that the "nose pressed against the window" is because of feelings of isolation early in life?

GOLDSMITH: I don't know what makes an artist. There are a lot of artists who've had rotten childhoods and a lot of artists who've had super-happy childhoods. The only thing that I would say all artists have in common, if they're really going to produce anything worthwhile, is that they remain vulnerable. You have to bare your heart and say, "Well, some people will say this is a nice heart and other people will stick an arrow in it." And that willingness to be vulnerable is the only thing I think artists have in common.

ZDENEK: But there must be some common motivation that makes all artists risk so much. It's not only the risk of artistic encounter, but it's also the risk of personal vulnerability—and being comfortable with that. It allows people to know you in a unique way.

GOLDSMITH: I always feel as if I'm peeling an onion and going deeper and deeper until the whole thing is exposed.

ZDENEK: When you feel apprehensive or anxious, is there any special way you deal with those feelings?

GOLDSMITH: When I'm apprehensive about something, I envision not the worst thing that could happen but the best thing that could happen. Somehow the euphoria of even the possibility that this wonderful thing could happen carries me right into the experience.

ZDENEK: It sounds almost like a visualization I do with my clients.

GOLDSMITH: It is a visualization.

ZDENEK: How far do you carry it?

GOLDSMITH: Right through until I'm not feeling the anxiety! I've really taught myself this trick. Let's say I'm seeing somebody who has a vital piece of information. When I first started in I would think, "Why would they give me this information? I'm never going to find this out. They would never tell me this." But people have told me things that were so incredible about themselves. Things you would never think anyone could extract from these hidden chests of secrets. And I think about all those things and I think, "Well, I really have a kind of key, and I'm going to go over there and this person is going to be able to tell me something they've never been able to tell anyone else. And aren't I going to feel fabulous? And aren't they going to feel wonderful having communicated this?"

ZDENEK: You gravitate to the memory of success and make it happen again. Some people gravitate to the memory of failure and spin downward.

GOLDSMITH: When a thing doesn't come immediately, the artist's instinct is to say, "Ah, it will never come. I've lost the magic." It's very difficult to give yourself the reinforcement, but you must do it. For example, Hemingway used to say that he wrote all day and he quit while the juice was up. He meant that if he quit while he was having a really good writing streak then he could go back the next morning in the middle of this really good writing and take off again. I can never do that. If I hit a really great writing streak, I think it's never going to come again; so I write till four or six in the morning till I'm too exhausted to write anymore. But to be able to take it one step further and to feel what Hemingway felt—well, that's the next thing I'm working toward.

ZDENEK: I think most writers feel the elusiveness of creativity, the elusiveness of the gift. When you're on a high and you're writing well, don't you get the feeling that the words are almost being written *through* you?

GOLDSMITH: Oh, yes, you're listening to your own music. I've done both fiction and non-fiction. And people will tell you that it's most important to listen to your own music when you're doing a novel because you're creating it from the inside. But I want to tell you it's just as important, or perhaps more important, in non-fiction.

You start with a bushel-basket of dry facts. To make that into the most beautiful cake you've ever concocted, you must have all these facts at your fingertips and then they must all blend together. And that is not all intellectual.

ZDENEK: What about dreams? Do you remember them?

GOLDSMITH: Well, I try to remember my dreams because they're one of the most valuable tools I have. If I don't remember them, I know I'm blocking something. I lose my dreams very, very quickly, so one of the things I do, whenever I can, is write them down first thing in the morning before I get out of bed. I must say there are a lot of mornings when I wake up and I don't have time to do that. But if I do, it's very helpful.

ZDENEK: Do you have any special way that you work with dreams?

GOLDSMITH: Well, the feeling of the dream is always useful, whether it's positive or negative. Even if you don't know how to read dreams in any complicated way—which I don't—I recall what I was feeling and that tells me a lot.

ZDENEK: Many writers get a disquieting feeling when they finish one book and haven't started another. In that period in between, some of us feel . . . well, terribly unsettled.

GOLDSMITH: Do you mean *desperate*?

ZDENEK: Really! Do you have any techniques that help you move on to the next work?

GOLDSMITH: Well, once you took me through a series of right-brain exercises that helped me realize what I *didn't* want to do. You asked me to write some fantasy experience, and what very clearly emerged out of that was that I did *not* want to do a project, a screenplay project, that had been offered to me. I was very tempted by the money, and I was in California and that would have been a very good place to do it. But I really didn't want to. Your exercise showed me that right away.

ZDENEK: It always helps to get in touch with what your right brain wants to do. That can really stimulate all kinds of creativity.

GOLDSMITH: I think all people can be in touch with their creativity. All people. And I think it will make their lives really brighter. You begin to look at things in a different way—things seem more beautiful, and life is just so much sweeter.

11

MARGE CHAMPION, Dancer/Choreographer

If you're in a hurry to get from New York City to Stockbridge, Massachusetts, there's a little tree-top airline whose planes are not really made of balsa wood—though you may want to look twice, just to be sure.

The motor started and rumbled and coughed and started again. In spite of the weight of my anxieties, the mini-plane lifted from the airstrip and skimmed just over the trees to follow the Hudson River north toward the Berkshires. Instinctively, I scanned the ground for a place to land—just in case. Beneath us the narrow river slipped through the trees, smooth as a long, dark satin ribbon, twisted and shimmering in the sun.

Along the shore, tall trees huddled close together, still green and lush, holding tenaciously to the tail of summer. But further north, the maples began to flush with color. The elms were golden, the oaks mottled and bold. It was not yet October; New England was a young girl ripe before her time.

When you don't have sisters or brothers, sometimes you choose your own family. For twenty-five years, Marge has been a special sister to me. We've co-authored a couple of books, co-produced some sizable liturgical celebrations, and I've seen her creativity at work in a myriad of situations.

Marge and Gower Champion were one of the most famous dance teams in America. After twenty-five years of marriage they went their separate ways—Gower to direct on Broadway and in films, Marge to choreograph "Queen of the Stardust Ballroom" (for which she won an Emmy) and to direct for the theater, to act again, and later to marry

115

the outstanding television director, Boris Sagal. After less than five years of marriage, Boris was killed in a helicopter accident—only months after Gower died of a rare blood disease.

There were many hours of talking before I put the tape recorder on the breakfast-room table and we started this interview. It was almost dawn.

Marge doesn't consciously use right-brain techniques, yet she is both creative and intuitive and her approach to problem-solving is wonderfully inventive. Affirmation comes naturally to her; it always has.

ZDENEK: I've learned a lot from you, Marge, about how to program success. You really *claim* success when you start a new project.

CHAMPION: Well, thinking in a positive way has a lot to do with my strong religious training. If you're on earth to affirm the glory of God, you can't do that by being negative.

ZDENEK: But you're even positive about the little things, like assuming you'll have a parking place in front of where you want to shop. What amazes me is how often that proves true.

CHAMPION: That's a wonderful game I've played all my life. If it's right for me to have an ice-cream cone, there will be a parking place in front of Baskin-Robbins. And if the parking place isn't there, well, I just stay open to whatever else presents itself.

ZDENEK: I've seen you take that same philosophical attitude with more major issues—from real estate to theater. You always expect things to work for you and, if they don't, you have a gift for discovering that something better is right around the corner.

CHAMPION: I've never had a major failure without having that failure lead to some kind of success.

ZDENEK: Can you give me a specific example?

CHAMPION: Sure . . . one has to do with Gower and myself. We were supposed to do a show in New York but we hadn't signed the contract yet. The backers had even raised all the money for the show. Then, through no fault of ours, the deal fell through. Well, that left us with nothing to do for the rest of the summer.

I guess it was my positive thinking that led us to take a job in California. We opened at the Mocambo—a club that was notorious for not always paying the performers. But it turned out to be great for us, because that step led right into our movie career.

ZDENEK: Between the moment you knew the show wasn't going to happen and the time you accepted the Mocambo deal, are you aware of how you dealt with the disappointment?

CHAMPION: Oh, yes. Oh, I'm definitely aware of that. I cry a little and I feel a bit of panic but I just don't wallow in it. I can't live like that. The only thing I think about is, "What have I learned from this?" I've learned I can go on. I can bounce back.

ZDENEK: Other than your spiritual philosophy, is there anything specific that helps you be so resilient?

CHAMPION: Strangely enough, dance helps me to overcome a lot of things. When I'm in class and the music is going, I'm in another space. My muscles are responding—sometimes not as happily as I'd like—but I'm drenched in perspiration and I'm in another space. And there is nothing important at that moment other than moving around to the music. It is a space that says, "This is where I should be at this very time." I have complete confidence in the rightness of that moment. So if things are jarring outside of that space, the class releases me from the responsibility of nitpicking to try to make things better. Then I feel so much more positive when I come out of class and usually, on the way home, I'll get an idea about how to solve a particular problem.

ZDENEK: You focus *away* from the problem so your unconscious can get a chance to work on the solution while you're dancing. And dancing is usually a right-brain activity.

CHAMPION: I don't know. But I know I come back with another perspective.

ZDENEK: You were talking before about how you program yourself to have success. In my terms that would be an example of *left*-hemisphere affirmation. Is there anything you do to program your *right* hemisphere and establish a positive feeling about success in non-verbal ways, such as visualization or fantasy?

CHAMPION: Not consciously. But the dreams I remember are always wonderfully successful. I rarely have nightmares or dream of something scary or unpleasant. My unconscious mind just celebrates success in my sleep.

And I never fantasize failure. I can't remember ever fantasizing how things feel when they go wrong. I never think about picking up the paper and seeing a rotten review.

ZDENEK: Did you ever fantasize picking up the paper and reading a really *good* review?

CHAMPION: Well, this is going to sound terrible, but I've been lucky enough to have such good reviews that I don't fantasize about that.

ZDENEK: You just expect the reviews to be good?

CHAMPION: I just expect everything to be okay. And the more work I do, the less I care about how one person, one reviewer, will react, and the more I care about how it will move a group of people. But if it should happen that a show is not good, I've learned that it is not the end of my life or my work. If something should go bad, I'm at a place I can look at it as a . . . a difficult . . . but a learning experience rather than something that would really shake me. Everything is not a matter of life and death.

ZDENEK: Not everyone has your natural expectation for success. In my work, I try to help people fantasize positive thoughts so they can use fantasy as a tool for thinking constructively.

CHAMPION: If you fantasize nothing but success, then you have to have some kind of mental trampoline so if it doesn't work out right you can let go of it. You have to let go of the times things don't go right. You can't just hug failure to you like a blanket. You need to jump out on the trampoline and say, "That was a bummer. Now, let's see how much I've learned and how much good is going to come out of that. How much higher can I go the next time?" I can hear myself saying to other people, "Yes, that was really a disappointment; it was really awful. Now it's bound to be better." I can also hear a lot of hooting and hollering from those people who are not willing to let go of disappointments.

ZDENEK: Letting go has always been one of your strong points. I remember when you and I went to New York to do "The Today Show" and I kept fretting because there was no guarantee that we would really go on the show. And I wanted to stay in the hotel room and wait for their call. And you said, "It's going to happen. Don't worry about it. And if it doesn't happen then something else will happen instead!" I've never forgotten that. At the time, I didn't understand how you could think that way but now I see how valuable that attitude is.

CHAMPION: I didn't negate the importance of that interview but I was able to release the anxiety.

ZDENEK: You have a wonderful ability to take a problem, lay it on the table, and walk off and do your business.

CHAMPION: When I can't do that—and there *are* times when I really can't let go—the only thing I do that quiets my mind is to pray. I'm careful to be real grateful the rest of the time because I have to let Him know, somehow, that it's not just when I'm in trouble that I keep in touch.

ZDENEK: I'm thinking about how you let go of losses. You have, in effect, lost two husbands in one year. When Boris was killed, you were still dealing with Gower's death, which was also a very sudden thing. And even though you and Gower were divorced, I know he was still a very important person to you.

CHAMPION: Yes, he was. And I not only lost two husbands in one year, I lost two partners. I had worked with both of them professionally, remember.

ZDENEK: Still, you move forward in your life. You haven't let grief stop you from making constructive choices. I know you've moved forward with your work. And in your personal life you've made positive decisions.

CHAMPION: I believe that we're the sum and substance of our previous experiences. When life hands you a series of blows you've got two choices—you can lie down and wallow in them or you can just go on. I mean, you have to deal with grief, you have to face it, but then you have to keep going on. I think I've just got too much pride to wallow in grief. This can either be something that stops you forever or it can be something that adds to your storehouse of experiences and emotional recall to prepare you for something that is bound to be around the corner.

ZDENEK: Being married to two terrific men and losing them still leaves you with the blessing that you had them and that they were a part of your life.

CHAMPION: And that all that happened in those years has gone into my "unconscious computer." I find so much of their influence coming out now, especially in the directing I'm doing. I'm constantly thinking, "Oh, thank you, Gower," or "Thank you, Boris, for that." It's all coming out as if it's original with me, but it's as if their talents rubbed off onto me; I've integrated both of them into who I am.

ZDENEK: I remember when you and Gower were divorced, you were determined to hold onto all the good things that you had shared together. You wouldn't negate the wonderful years by focusing on the things that caused you to divorce. It takes a lot of maturity to hold to all that was good without denying the things that were wrong. That's about the best use of affirmation that I know.

CHAMPION: Oh, you have to do that. You have to. That year they died, I lost all of my jewelry, and all of my personal mementos were stolen from the house—the things that belonged to Gower's mother and the silver samovar Boris's mother brought from Russia. All kinds of things—even the ring Boris bought me when we married.

That was the year everybody went away. Everything was taken. Maybe that's why it was easy for me to move out of Los Angeles and come to Stockbridge, to the country. I wasn't running away but I was moving to a protected place. A different environment. I mean, even the Lord Himself went off into the desert— not because of loss, but to think things through, to pray. It seemed to me that I needed to do that. And to quietly take care of my grief. And I began to find great healing power in just being really aware of the landscape. Of the taste of the water I was drinking. Of the clearness of the air. Of noticing everything and being thankful for all that was good.

ZDENEK: When you are so aware of those sensory things, what does that do for you?

CHAMPION: It feels like I've been away in a very complicated space for a long time and I've gotten back into a kind of basic, almost primal space. Taking care of the snow and seeing the first buds coming up in the spring and all of that just helps me get centered. It happens in California but not so dramatically. It's all kind of homogenized there. Whereas in the country, it's the cream on the top of the milk. Those first crocuses that come up are fighting their way through and you're so aware of it. And in the summer, you're so aware of those fireflies on those warm, wet summer nights. It's the old cliché, I guess. "Take time to smell the roses." But when you've been living very fast and a lot has been happening to you it helps to be in a place like this. There's such a celebration of the seasons: The Oktoberfest that goes on so long, and Christmas is Christmas—not like it is with palm trees—and then spring comes 'round.

ZDENEK: You're using the experience of the senses, not just for creativity but for survival. That's a viable problem-solving device: to use all that is good around you to help you get over the pain. Do you daydream a lot?

CHAMPION: I'm not sure I know what daydreaming really is. I don't think I do what most people call daydreaming. But I sit in that window and look out over that whole forest of the Berkshires and watch every sunset until it gets dark. I look out over that view, and I find it the most warming, wonderful experience. But I don't go off into a fantasy of what it would be like to sit there with . . . anyone. I don't have conscious thoughts. No memories or plans. I'm busy letting that landscape fill my eyes and I just listen to the silence. I'm so busy doing that, I never think of anything except what is right before me.

ZDENEK: You really live the moment. How long do you do that each day?

CHAMPION: About an hour. Sometimes that time makes me very happy and sometimes it makes me extremely sad. Even to the point of tears. Sometimes it's an overwhelming feeling of loneliness. Or an overwhelming feeling of abundance.

ZDENEK: And yet you're not conscious of the thoughts that stir those feelings?

CHAMPION: Not really. I used to toast the sunset every evening. And then I found that I didn't want even that small amount of alcohol. I didn't want anything that would alter the way things really are.

That hour when I watch the sunset, I'm the richest person. I just feel very appreciative of all that is good.

PART III

YOUR
PERSONAL
PROGRAM

Introduction

How to Use
Your Personal Program

There are several ways you can use the exercise section of *The Right-Brain Experience*:

1. You can work with a friend, each of you taking turns as the "enabler." It is important that the person with whom you work be someone you can trust, for you'll be dealing with some very personal material in this program. Of course, you can decide not to reveal what you have written, but most people have a very strong desire to discuss the results of the exercises. In any case, I suggest you choose your partner with great care.

2. You can work with a group. One benefit of a group is that the role of "enabler" can be shared by several people. Working with others compounds the problem of confidentiality but provides an opportunity for more varied support and encouragement. There are only two rules in my class: No one has to do anything she (he) doesn't want to do (such as perform a specific exercise or share extremely personal insights that are realized during an exercise); and no one can "critique" another's material in an unkind way. To function well, the group must not operate like an encounter group; its purpose is to provide an atmosphere of safety and affirmation.

3. You can work alone and tape the visualization exercises prior to your work time. That enables you to relax, enjoy the experience, and gain maximum benefit from the material.

4.   You can order the professional tapes I have made, which use not only the voice but ocean sounds and meditative music as well.

5.   You can read each exercise until you are thoroughly familiar with the sequence of suggestions; then you can perform the visualizations without tape machines or help from another person.

Weigh the advantages of each approach and choose the way that works best for you.

To do the right-brain exercises properly, it is most important to prepare three things:

Setting: Find a quiet place where you won't be disturbed by friends, family, pets, phone, or doorbell. Try to protect yourself from any distraction that could break your concentration and shatter the mood. Choose a place where you feel peaceful and private. It may be in your home—or perhaps even in your car, parked in a beautiful secluded setting. Give serious thought to your ideal work space; privacy is extremely important to this experience.

Time: This program has been designed to be done for two consecutive hours over a period of six days. (If that is difficult for you, it is possible to devise an alternate plan.) To get the most from this program, establish *exactly* when you plan to work and honor that commitment. The effect of these exercises is cumulative, so try to work in blocks of time and, if possible, work on consecutive days.

Equipment: You'll need a pencil or pen and a notebook to be used only for this experience. If you have a tape recorder, it will be useful; a kitchen timer or alarm clock is also useful for timing some of the exercises that are best performed at high speed while working "against the clock."

This notebook will be very personal. Many of the things that come to your mind may be quite revealing—emotional honesty is invaluable for the full effectiveness of the program. So don't be hesitant to write things down. Consider this your journal or diary for your own intimate account of right-brain insights. You'll find it interesting to come back to these pages a month from now or a year from now and observe the changes that have taken place in your life.

At first, use this book as you would a cookbook, following the recipes carefully. Later, you can begin to improvise and create new exercises. Once you understand how the right brain functions and experience the procedure for getting its cooperation, you can develop your own exercises to meet your specific needs.

It is also helpful, for long range use, to begin to notice times and situations that stimulate your creativity. As imaginative ideas come to you, notice the circumstances that triggered the idea. Where were you? What were you doing? What were you feeling? What were you thinking? After periods of high creativity, try to look back and write down the circumstances. Learn to be attentive to the moment. Be aware of times when you "see" more clearly.

Through self-awareness and the experiences provided by these exercises, you are learning to tame the wild creative energy that exists in your right brain; you are learning to harness the power that will soon be within your control.

12

The First Day

Awareness Chart

Many people are so out of touch with their bodies and their emotions that they have trouble defining exactly what they feel at a given time. The Awareness Chart will trace what you are feeling at the beginning of each day's work and will give you a reference point for evaluating your progress through this course.

On your chart you will represent your emotional state by means of numbers. A zero (0) represents a state of deep relaxation, an open mind, and a sense of expectancy and receptivity. The negative side of the scale (-10 to -1) indicates degrees of negative energy; negative energy expresses itself through feeling emotionally or creatively "blocked," experiencing nervous tension, or thinking in a rigid, narrow way. (Negative ten indicates the most extreme state of these conditions.)

The positive side of the scale ($+1$ through $+10$) reflects an increase in productive and innovative feelings and approaches that powerful state known as a "creative high." (Feelings of ecstasy and positive energy occur toward the $+10$ end of the scale.)

To sustain a high degree of creativity over an extended period of time, it is valuable to know how to return to a relaxed condition periodically. You need to pace yourself if you're working under a deadline on a long project. Developing the ability to determine your mental and

AWARENESS CHART

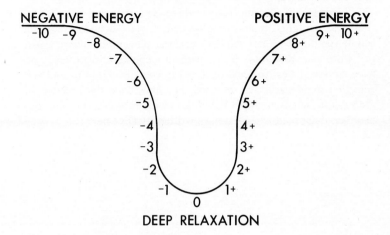

NEGATIVE ENERGY   **POSITIVE ENERGY**

-10 -9 -8
-7
-6
-5
-4
-3
-2
-1   0   1+
2+
3+
4+
5+
6+
7+
8+ 9+ 10+

DEEP RELAXATION

physical condition allows you to work for long periods of time in a highly productive state without burning up your energy.

Study the chart and try to get an accurate sense of which number most accurately reflects what you are feeling at this very moment. Put a circle around the number that shows what you are feeling right now.

If you find it difficult to define what you are feeling, be patient with yourself. This is not always easy to do. Take your time and understand that this type of evaluation will become increasingly easier as you progress through the program.

NEGATIVE ENERGY	POSITIVE ENERGY
feeling blocked	feeling productive
thinking in a rigid style	thinking in an innovative style
awareness of nervous tension	awareness of a "creative high"

What Your Left Brain Thinks About You

The purpose of this exercise is to provide a "base of operations" to determine your pre-conceived image of yourself. Later, when you look back, you will have a clear picture of your attitudes at the beginning of this program.

Speed is critical to this exercise because we are trying to capture your *first* thoughts; taking time to analyze your answers would be counter-productive. After you have read this paragraph, take your pen and write your thoughts quickly without stopping to read what you have written. Later, you will be asked to come back to this and you will then understand its relevance. For now, trust the process. In grocery-list fashion, make a list of the words *that describe you.* Remember, don't read what you have written! Ready? Begin.

1.	9.
2.	10.
3.	11.
4.	12.
5.	13.
6.	14.
7.	15.
8.	16.

I know it's tempting but please *don't read the list of words*—just turn the page and move on.

CATEGORY 1.
OUTSMARTING THE LEFT BRAIN

Mandala # 1

The mandala on the next page is more than a simple pattern; it is your first step toward control of your creative hemisphere. During the time you focus on the mandala, your verbal left brain will become frustrated because it can't deal with spatial relationships and it will stop paying attention. Then your right brain can begin to take over.

The mandala will help you find the silence that lies deep within you.

Sit comfortably in your chair and hold the drawing before you. Focus on the center of the figure and observe the pattern. You don't need to "think" about the drawing at all, only to "feel" the sensations caused by the pattern. Plan to stare at the center of that paper as long as you feel comfortable doing so. The visual patterns will seem to shift

as you concentrate on the center. Most people begin by spending five or ten minutes on this exercise; some students find that an even longer period is helpful.

The mandala will help you to:

- center your attention
- quiet the chattering of your inner dialogue
- distract the left hemisphere, which cannot deal with spatial relationships
- allow the right hemisphere to dominate for an extended period of time

Results From This Right-Brain Experience

You will begin to feel more relaxed and more "centered" after this exercise. The simplicity of it is disarming but the effects are highly beneficial.

There are some people, however, who find that after a few minutes they feel restless and have trouble concentrating. They should realize that it is quite all right to work at their own pace. Even a few moments each day will help the mind stop its fluttering pattern. Almost everyone is comfortable with the mandala after the third day and finds it extremely beneficial.

CATEGORY 2.
BIOFEEDBACK TRAINING

A Classic Beginning

Your body responds dramatically to your thoughts. Thoughts are powerful and, to a great extent, determine how your body functions. Thoughts can make your blood pressure rise—directing them can bring your blood pressure down. Thoughts can create blocks that stifle your creativity—learning to direct your thoughts can release the power that is already within you. If your thoughts have made you tense, the power of your mind can allow your body to relax.

This warm-up exercise will help you attain the zero rating on the Awareness Chart. Once you become expert at using your mental powers to control your body energy, you will be able to reach a state of deep relaxation very quickly. In the beginning, it will take longer— perhaps even a few days of practice—before you are able to "let go" of all the destructive tension held in your body. But, paradoxically, the harder you try, the more difficult the task will be. The secret is in not trying but in *allowing* your body to release the tension. Be kind to yourself and know that it doesn't matter whether you achieve a deeply-relaxed state today, tomorrow, or the next day; the important thing is that you are on the right path. Feel free to progress at whatever speed corresponds to your natural rhythm for these exercises.

Choose the most comfortable place in the room to sit. (If you lie down, you might get so relaxed you will fall asleep.) It's best to uncross your legs and avoid any position that produces tension. Loosen any clothing that binds you. Let your arms lie comfortably by your side.

How does the surface beneath you feel against your body?

> Soft . . . (Are plush cushions pressing against you?)
> Cool . . . (Is smooth wood touching your skin?)

As you close your eyes,

> follow the transition to darkness . . .
> halos of light . . .
> fading slowly . . .
> a black screen.

Without changing its pattern, listen to your breathing.

> Is it easy and relaxed?

Put your hand on your abdomen and take a deep breath.

> If you are breathing well,
> that breath should make your hand lift
> as your chest and abdomen expand.

Try again now . . .

> Feel the difference?

Very slowly, count to five as you take a deep breath and hold it
for five more counts and *slowly* exhale through your mouth.
One . . . two . . . three . . . four . . . five.

That probably made you yawn,
for you are starting to relax.

Take one more deep breath, continuing to count and relax.

One . . . two . . . three . . . four . . . five . . .
hold . . . and exhale.

Imagine a spot that is the center of your body. Try to scrunch all
of your muscles toward that center. Every muscle of your body should
tighten as you try to reach that center point.

Now relax.
Be aware of the *feeling* of
tension and relaxation.

Think of that same center point and try to *stretch* all your muscles
away from that point. Stretch as far away from that center as you can.

And relax.

Notice the very subtle sensation that moves through your body.
Focus all your attention on your feet and tighten their muscles as
much as you can.

tighten . . . two . . . three . . . four . . . five . . .
hold . . . two . . . three . . . four . . . five . . .
relax . . . two . . . three . . . four . . . five . . .

Now, be aware of your ankles and stretch them

tighten . . . two . . . three . . . four . . . five . . .
hold . . . two . . . three . . . four . . . five . . .
relax . . . two . . . three . . . four . . . five . . .

And of your calves

tighten . . . two . . . three . . . four . . . five . . .
hold . . . two . . . three . . . four . . . five . . .
relax . . . two . . . three . . . four . . . five . . .

And of your thighs

tighten . . . two . . . three . . . four . . . five . . .
hold . . . two . . . three . . . four . . . five . . .
relax . . . two . . . three . . . four . . . five . . .

Be aware of your buttocks and pull them tight, make them hard

for the count of five
hold . . .
and relax . . . two . . . three . . . four . . . five . . .

Arch your back now

stretching like a cat
hold . . . two . . . three . . . four . . . five . . .
relax . . . two . . . three . . . four . . . five . . .

Press your shoulders forward

as far as they want to go
hold . . .
relax . . .

Press your shoulders backward

stretching . . .
holding . . .
relaxing . . .

Make your arms stiff as they can be

hold . . .
relax . . .

Move your wrists in slow even circles

rotating . . .
holding . . .
relaxing . . .

Curl your fingers

and stretch . . .
and hold . . .
and relax . . .

Move your neck in a slow circle

> all the way around
> you can feel the muscles pull
> and relax . . .

Tighten your face . . .

> hold . . .
> and relax . . .

Take a deep breath . . .

> and let it go.

Stretch any part of your body that wants to be stretched.

> Take another deep breath

And suggest to yourself that your right brain wants to help you reach your goals. Tell your right brain that you want to be more creative and you welcome its help.

> Slowly, very slowly, open your eyes
> and consider how you feel.

From the Awareness Chart on p. 129 write in your notebook the number that best describes how you are feeling now.

The left side of your brain is not at all interested in what you have just been doing.

> Your right hemisphere was in charge during most of this experience in body awareness.

**Results From This
Right-Brain Experience**

Your mind has just directed your body to relax and your body has responded to the suggestion. In my seminars we see lots of smiles and a few yawns and some contented stretches after this exercise.

There are some people, however, whose bodies won't respond to their mind's suggestions. Some people have never learned how to relax at all—certainly not at times of their own choosing. I encourage them to continue to try and if, at the end of six sessions, they still have trouble conditioning their bodies to relax, I recommend some sessions with a biofeedback machine, not only for the value it brings to this program, but for reasons of general health. People who cannot relax under any circumstances usually have some physical symptoms that indicate their body's inability to release tension. Many ulcer patients and those who complain of chronic neck and back pain fit into this category.

CATEGORY 3.
GUIDED VISUALIZATION

In Distant Woods

If you are working alone on this program and have not recorded this exercise on tape (or ordered the professional tapes; see the Appendix), then it is important for you to work in "sections." Read until you come to a natural stopping point. Then close your eyes and *recall* the instructions.

Imagine that you are walking alone in the woods. The trees are lush and beautiful.

Can you see them? (Or "sense" their presence?)
Imagine the colors . . . bring them clearly into focus in your "mind's eye."
Listen to the sounds . . .
Notice the smell of the trees . . .
How does the air feel against your skin?

There is a narrow stream running nearby. Enjoy the sound of rushing water for a moment. Now, cross to the other side by stepping on the large, flat stones that protrude above the water.

Walk slowly through the forest until you come to a beautiful meadow, where you sit down to rest. Be intensely aware of what you see and feel.

Are the colors different here? The sounds?

Sit quietly for awhile and notice the specific details of the meadow. Create the scene as clearly as you can.
There is a sound at the edge of the forest.
What is the sound?

When you are ready to leave the meadow, walk deeper into the heart of the forest. Be aware of the sound of your feet upon the path.

Define the texture of the ground beneath your step.

Move around a bend in the path and discover a house not far away in a clearing.

Were you surprised to find it there?

(Perhaps you really knew it was there all the time.)

Write a description of the *outside* of the house in your notebook. Move closer and discover that the door is slightly open. It is all right to enter the house; you are not intruding. Step inside and be aware that you are alone. Look around. What do you see? Write your description of the room in your notebook.

There is a window open at the front of the house. Look out the window and write what you see. Explore the house. Wander through the rooms, down the dark hallway to the closed door at the end. Open the door and look inside. At first you think the room is empty but then you see a child sleeping in a small bed in the alcove. Imagine what the child feels when you come in. What does the child want to say to you? Write what the child says and what you say (or want to say) in return.

Is there anything about the child's response that reminds you of your own feelings? If so, ask yourself if that feeling has been hovering around your subconscious for some time. If you were to put that emotion into one word, what would that word be?

If you felt any strong emotion emerge from your time in that house and want to work with the feeling, use a page in your notebook to express that emotion more clearly. You might write a poem, draw a picture, compose a melody. Don't work for perfection in this space (your critic is out to lunch, remember). Let the power of the emotions direct your words.

Results From This Right-Brain Experience

Dr. Robert Good always wanted to write; and he said he had done so in the past with some success. His goal was to break the writer's block that had troubled him for years. The first day of class, after the warm-up exercises of spatial confusion and biofeedback, I led my students through the same guided visualization that you have just completed.

One of the most touching experiences we shared that day, as people read what they had just written, was one single line written by Bob. He described the house in the woods in sparse terms, indicating that around the house there was laughter and children playing. Then he wrote this one line: "On my side of the posted fence, I stand and yearn."

Bob read his words in a low, quiet voice, almost a whisper. The eloquence in that line comes not only from what was said, but from what was withheld. It was left to others to imagine what happened to a child to make him feel so apart from the nourishing love of a family—and to recall that pain so vividly as a mature adult.

Bob said very little for the next four days of class but he worked every exercise. Then, on the last day, he told us he had broken his writer's block. He had written a story filled with complexity and passion. Furthermore, he knew the exact title and the theme for a book he wanted to write.

Rose Cabe said she had never written a poem. I found that hard to believe but she was emphatic. Not in school, not in her childhood diary, never—not that she could recall. She told us that she couldn't write poetry, that her left brain had led her to more "practical" work.

But, during this exercise, when Rose encountered the child in the room she saw a memory of her own child in her crib. Suddenly, Rose recalled two powerful events of her life—the birth of her child and the death of her mother. She took the exact words that were said to her at those times and placed them in juxtaposition as lyrics for a folk song. The words seemed to write themselves:

Rose, you have a daughter. Rose, your mother's gone.
In our beginnings and our endings, we hear life's holy song.

All of life is holding on—and then it's letting go.
There is a struggle in between, because I love them so.

There's got to be a pattern in the fabric on the loom,
Seen from a greater distance—only death can give us room.

Rose, you have a daughter. Rose, your mother's gone.
In the multicolored fabric, we see life's holy song.

Later that week, composer/performer Paul Bergen set Rose's words to music and sang them, with guitar accompaniment, at a meeting of the Santa Barbara Writers Conference.

CATEGORY 4.
TRANSITIONAL OBJECTS

You Can Go Home Again

Take a deep breath, hold it, then slowly exhale. Any time you choose to do this particular kind of breathing, it will remind you of th Conditioned Relaxation from the biofeedback exercise. And you can gradually learn to allow that one deep breath to carry you instantly into that deeply-relaxed state.

If any parts of your body need to stretch, stretch them now. Let go of any tension that has returned to you. And close your eyes.

Let your thoughts scan the early years of your life. Some people have trouble remembering so far back; others return to the past quite easily. Perhaps it will help if you think of something that mattered very much to you then; was there a doll, a toy, a blanket? What did you have that mattered most of all? If you have difficulty with this, perhaps you can think of the house you lived in when you first started school. Let your imagination carry you back inside that house to your bedroom. *Now* can you find that special object that mattered so much to you? Take time to find that significant item before you move on.

Let that memory carry you to other recollections. You may recall faces, feelings, events . . . Let your mind drift across the images. Let your mind see . . . feel . . . relive that time.

Go back to the first time you remember sitting in a classroom. Were you near the front? The back? The right side of the room or the left?

> The desk in front of you was probably made of wood. Was it scarred? Were names carved there? Did you ever trace your finger along the lines of the pencil tray or the knife cuts?

Who is sitting in front of you? Are there colors that you recall? Do you remember the teacher?

If you seem to remember a classroom from one age and a teacher from another age, no matter; people often condense several memories into one. You are looking for the *feelings* of your childhood more than the facts. All memory is fiction. Who can remember exactly how it was? It is your inner truths that are of interest to us now.

Write whatever memories come to mind. You may want to write as you would in recording a dream, letting your sentences move from thought to thought, jumping from one situation to another.

If for some reason, you simply cannot recall your early childhood, then imagine a childhood for yourself, and make up the story. How do you imagine your life was then? Write the first memories that come to mind—a single event or fragments of memories, whichever you choose.

Can you remember a secret from your childhood? Something you promised never to tell? Who told you the secret?

What was it about?

Were you tempted to tell someone?

Did you tell someone?

What happened then?

Remember the first time you discovered that your parents kept secrets from you? Do you remember how you felt? Was there one important secret you discovered? Do you remember it now?

Can you remember the first time you saw a naked child of the opposite sex? What did you think? What did you feel?

Who was your best friend in gradeschool?

What was the best thing about that friend?

What was the most wonderful thing you ever did together?

And what else does that lead you to remember?

Do these memories help you get in touch with the child that is a part of you still? Treat that child, and the memories, with great respect. Be sure that the adult part of yourself has a nurturing attitude toward the child that you were/are and, in some ways, will always be.

Is there some specific thing you wish someone had said to you when you were a child?

If you had the power to turn time back and to re-write the past, is there some memory that comes to mind that you wish you could alter? Be very still and let the story unfold in fantasy. Let the child hear or feel what is needed. Let the child be comforted or strengthened by what happens in this new ending to an old event.

CATEGORY 5.
OTHER-HAND WRITING

What Your Right Brain
Feels About You

This exercise is specifically designed for your non-dominant hand. Take your pen in the hand you *don't* write with. You will probably find it difficult to write legibly and may even feel a little silly. Bear with me—this is important. Now write, in grocery-list fashion, all the words you feel describe you. *Don't stop to think*—that is most important. Quickly, start writing your list.

1.	9.
2.	10.
3.	11.
4.	12.
5.	13.
6.	14.
7.	15.
8.	16.

Now, read the list and compare your words with the list you made with your other hand. You will probably see how much more vulnerable your left-hand (right-brain) list reveals you to be.

Results From This
Right-Brain Experience

If you are clearly right-handed (not just in writing, but in every-thing) this list-making will probably reveal great differences in the self-assessment by each hemisphere. If you have had a great deal of psychotherapy or have been using other forms of right-brain stimulation, the right-brain list and left-brain list will be more similar. This is because your right brain has previously communicated those private feelings to the "other side." You probably discovered that your first list (dominant hand) revealed characteristics you generally acknowledge. But your left-hand (non-dominant hand) list probably revealed surprising vulnerability. You may be shocked by what your unconscious mind leads your left hand to reveal.

A typical example of this exercise is from a Florida woman, who is about thirty-five and quite attractive.

The first list (dominant hand):

honorable, wondering, pretty, warm, loving, caring, giving, wanting, worker, impatient.

The second list (non-dominant hand):

generous, angry, scared, dreamer, hoping, needing, crying, sad, silly, lonely, tortured, fragmented.

Sometimes the lists have similar words. This is called the echo effect: the first list often makes itself heard in the early part of the second. Then the more vulnerable words appear.

Were the words of your two lists as extreme as the example? If so, then your unconscious has kept many secrets from you. These secrets will gradually be revealed as you progress through the program.

CATEGORY 6.
SENSORY STIMULATION

Retraining Your Senses

This first exercise in sensory stimulation is very general and covers all five senses (six, if you have the gift!). On other days, specific exercises will focus on one of the senses for a longer period. Today, we will touch briefly on all of them.

Concentrate intently on the following suggestions. Take your time. There's no hurry with this exercise.

Here and now, I am aware of:

The gift of sight. Choose one thing in the room and look at it in a new way, as a child would look at a fascinating new object. Using only your eyes, explore its contours, its details. Try to look with fresh eyes, to discover something about it you have never seen before.

The gift of hearing. Choose one sound and hear it in a new way. Are there noises outside? Experience them as new sounds. Is there nothing but silence? Turn on some music or any machine. One student sat on the kitchen floor, turned on the dishwasher, and discovered that the sounds of whirling water and sloshing noises stirred the imagination. She could actually use those sounds constructively by focusing intensely on what she was hearing. I once used a passing train for a "here-and-now" class exercise and found it to be a fascinating experience. Imagine the slow, mournful wail in the distance, building to a great crescendo with sub-dominant noises as part of the chorus, and then the sudden dropping off of sound.

The gift of smell. Are there any odors in the room? Can you smell flowers or perfume? Something from the kitchen? The scent of cedar burning in the fireplace or pipe tobacco or leather? Consciously imprint that scent into your mind as if you were trying to remember it.

The gift of taste. Is there a taste in your mouth that you can define? Is it sweet? Metallic? Pleasant? Open your mouth and yawn. Now be aware of your mouth and the taste that is there.

The gift of touch. With your left hand, rub your fingers across the back of your right hand. Feel the texture of the skin, the contours of veins and bones. Be aware of something new about your hand. Close your eyes and draw your finger across the back of your hand as if you were sketching it in your mind.

Sit quietly for a moment and see if any new awareness comes to your mind. Any feeling or sensation or thought? If so, write it down. If not, let it be . . . and move on.

CATEGORY 7.
FANTASY

Re-creation

Your ability to fantasize is based on your ability to play with imagination. This exercise incorporates the use of the senses, of memory, and of fantasy. If you have a well-developed ability to visualize, this will seem extremely easy to you. If you have difficulty creating mental pictures, perhaps you would like to keep this exercise tucked away in your mind and try it several times during the day to help develop this ability. Once you see how easily you can re-create memory, it's only one simple step to playing creatively with images and stimulating any kind of right brain activity you want to experience.

> Imagine a movie screen and project the images I suggest onto the white screen.
> Think of projecting *outward,* not onto the dark screen of closed lids.

Close your eyes and visualize a red apple. Is the color bright and the surface shiny? Is the stem broken or intact? Consider the color . . . can you make it a brighter red?

> Take the apple in your hand and feel its smoothness. Is it firm or is it over-ripe? Are there bruises? Feel all around the apple and notice if there are any soft spots or blemishes. Take a bite out of the apple. Can you taste it? Can you define the texture? If you are hungry, take another bite and let it satisfy your need.

Now visualize an orange. Is your orange large and thick-skinned like a navel orange—or small and smooth in texture like the Valencia? Can you make the color more vivid?

> Touch the orange and feel the texture. Begin peeling the skin. You can put the peelings on the napkin you visualize beside your chair. Open the body of the orange and pull a segment away from the rest and put it in your mouth. Is the taste of it sweet? Are there seeds? Is it juicy or perhaps more firm? Take a warm, damp cloth from your imagination and wipe your hands.

There are two bunches of grapes on a table that stands before you in your mind's eye. One bunch of grapes is green and seedless. The other is deep purple. Can you clearly see the colors? Notice the difference in the sizes. Can you make the green grapes slightly smaller in size and the purple ones just a bit larger?

> Remove one green grape and sense the tension that holds it to its stem, as it resists when you pull. Now pick one purple grape. Which one clung more tenaciously to the stem?

> Eat the green grape first and enjoy the taste. Now the purple one—but watch out for the seeds.

Both a lemon and a lime are on a plate. Compare the shades of yellow and green.

Feel the difference in the textures. Are they ripe or beginning to spoil?

Are you dreading what you think is coming next?

Maybe you don't want to taste either the lemon or the lime. If you don't want to, don't taste it. But you might want to *remember* the taste and be aware of your resistance and the excess of saliva, or you may feel that you've had quite enough of this exercise and would like to move on.

Which it is time to do, anyway.

Results From This Right-Brain Experience

A client of mine from San Francisco reported in a private session her experience with the re-creation exercise:

"I couldn't see any of the fruit. Some of the colors, yes, but not all of them, and they kept slipping away. I couldn't taste anything at all."

"What have you been feeling lately?" I asked her, knowing that she has been widowed little more than a year. Her children are grown and live in different cities; there have been many changes in her life in the last twelve months.

"I feel sort of . . . dead inside. Withdrawn. I can't see any way out. I can't imagine what to do to change any of this. Nothing seems good anymore. I have no appetite for anything."

We talked about some choices she could make that might help her deal more effectively with grief and depression. She agreed that a psychiatrist I recommended might help her discover even more options. The next time we met, she had less difficulty visualizing, although it was never as easy for her as it is for most people. Nonetheless, there was some progress both in terms of her ability to create pictures in her imagination and to deal constructively with her personal problems. How much of this successful outcome was because of this program, and how much was because of psychotherapy would be impossible to determine.

CATEGORY 8.
DREAM WORK

Listen to the Dreamer

Think back to last night and imagine yourself asleep in bed. Can you recall any dreams? Take a moment to consider this and see if some fragments of memory begin to surface. Write down the dream, using the present tense: "I see . . ." is much more effective than "I saw . . ." Try to *re-live* the dream. If you really can't recall one, make one up and write it in your notebook.

Try to recapture the mood of the dream. Close your eyes and experience the feeling; use the memory-triggering device of sensory stimulation (colors, sounds, textures, etc.). After a few minutes write down your associations to the dream. Whatever thoughts come to mind about anything at all are important. Write fast and in phrases or broken thoughts, using flashes of images—whatever the dream reminds you of now. Let your mind roll free, and write whatever thoughts, feelings, or recollections catch on the emotions that surface from working with the dream. Write as quickly as the ideas come to mind.

Results From This
Right-Brain Experience

B.J., age forty-seven, reported this dream to a small group who gathered in my home.

The dream: "I am furious with my daughter in the dream. I scream at her but she won't listen. I plead with her but she keeps on ignoring me. She is quitting an executive job with a prestigious advertising firm to be somebody's maid. I tell her that doesn't make any sense. She acts like she can't hear me."

Her association: "It seems really obvious what I'm upset about. In real life, my daughter just bought a large house and she is going to have to work very hard to make the payments. I'm worried about the time it will cost her to clean such a large place. I guess I'm afraid that she is 'giving up' too much money from her job for mortgage payments and giving up valuable leisure time to do all that housework."

Her further associations: "I think the person in the dream wasn't my daughter at all—it was really me. I have a career that doesn't pay much but it's very important to me, very satisfying. I work on my own schedule and so many people keep expecting me to quit work to take care of their needs. I think I've been angry about that for a very long time. I take care of other people's tedious chores and give up my own work to do that. I've been aware of resenting this but I never listened to myself, not *really* listened. In my dream, I guess I heard myself screaming to *me* to stop doing all those chores at the expense of my job. I couldn't hear how angry I felt about it until now. I do have a choice, but I've been acting like I don't. I mean, I don't *have* to keep on being at everyone's beck and call."

Follow-up: She finally *heard* her right-brain suggestions and demanded (of herself first, and her family later) that she have a certain number of hours for her work. No one could disturb her—unless there was a real emergency. She loved her family very much and found that she enjoyed helping them when she realized that her own needs would be met also.

Special Instructions
for Dream Work Categories 1–6

Since the recording of dreams and the free association to dreams is most effective in the early morning hours, try to record your dreams as soon after you awaken as possible. Starting tonight, put a pen and paper beside your bed. Each morning, write your dream and your associations to it *before getting out of bed.* You will get maximum benefit from this exercise if you catch your right-brain signals before your left brain is fully awake.

If you can't take the time in the early morning to write out your entire dream, see if you can capture at least a phrase or two and write it down. Then use those notes to stimulate your memory of the dream during your regular work period.

If your dream simply refuses to be recalled, then *imagine* a dream you might have had and play with the ideas that come to mind.

CATEGORY 9.
FREE ASSOCIATION

Morning Wisdom # 1

This is a timed exercise. If you have a clock, set it for ten minutes. You'll need your notebook.

Effective free-association techniques work best when there is no "consultation" with the left hemisphere while you are writing. Don't read the material back or slow down to think. Just record the phrases, thought fragments, or anything else that is triggered by letting the right brain spin in any direction it wants to go. Remember, you are not trying to write a well-formed paper, you are just laying out some fly paper to catch any unconscious awareness that might land on this page.

When you finish, *don't review what you have written.* It is important to do this exercise every day for six days without looking at any of the results. On the sixth day, you'll read all of the exercises at one sitting. Instructions for how to interpret and benefit from this material will be given in detail on the last day. For now, please resist the temptation to read what you write. Trust the process. Your right brain knows what to do.

CATEGORY 10.
GIFTS FROM THE RIGHT BRAIN

Awareness Summary # 1

Toward the close of each day's work-time, it's helpful to take stock of what these exercises have led you to discover.

1. From on the Awareness Chart, (p. 129) record in your notebook the number that best defines what you are feeling now.

2. Are you aware of specific feelings or insights that came to you as a result of working these exercises? If so, make some notes to yourself about that. If not, don't be harsh with yourself; some people have years of hardened defenses encrusting their feelings, and it takes hours of chipping at the protective surface before the treasures are revealed.

3. Did you recognize some dragons that were hanging around in the right side of your brain? If so, name them. If not, be assured that you do have dragons residing there and they will approach you in their own good time. When you can face them and call them by name, they will be much less disruptive to your dreams as well as far less influential in your waking life.

4. Did you get in touch with the child that has been hiding inside you for all your adult years? Do you see a relationship between the feelings that were stirred by your imagination and feelings that you still deal with as an adult?

5. Between now and the next time you open this book, be aware of sudden gestalts and ideas that seem to come "out of the blue." You have stirred some forces that may choose to express themselves later today. Be aware of them. You can use them effectively in tomorrow's work.

6. It is important to remember that you may be feeling more vulnerable than usual after working these exercises. If you are uncomfortable with that vulnerability, you can choose to "close down" your receptiveness to right-brain input. Balancing your bankbook or adding any long column of figures will get you back in left-brain mode. You might even alphabetize some words from a page of your favorite magazine. (You'll get bored with that very quickly, but it will start your linear, logical left hemisphere stirring again.) Be sure to complete Category 11 before consciously stimulating left-brain assertiveness.

Remember the importance of continuity in this program. The exercises are cumulative and work most effectively in sequence. Breaks between work days will set you back, so try to work on six *consecutive* days, if you can.

CATEGORY 11.
AFFIRMATIONS

Programming Success

This last exercise of the day is a present you can give yourself, a reward for a good day's work. Some people think of it as a blessing, for it will make you feel very good about yourself and your potential.

Affirmations are extremely simple, direct, and effective. The verbal affirmation will instruct your left hemisphere and the imaging affirmations will program your right hemisphere. It is important that both sides of your brain believe that success can become a reality and is, in fact, already in process.

On this first day, the affirmation is designed to help you realize that you are a unique, creative, imaginative person. You were born with the capacity to be creative and you are now experiencing the full realization of that fact.

Read the following affirmation and imagine your name in the three blank spaces:

I, _____, was born with the capacity to be creative.

You, _____, were born with the capacity to be creative.

She (He), _____, was born with the capacity to be creative.

The first sentence is a statement by your adult-self affirming your abilities. The second sentence may remind you of the voice of someone close to you; in your imagination, this could be the voice of any person who is very important in your life and whose opinions you value. Think of the third sentence as praise from people who have had authority over you or people you have tried hard to please.

Say the affirmation aloud, allowing the words to imprint themselves upon your mind. You may want to write them on 3 × 5 index cards and put them around the house. Many people collect affirmations and remember to say them several times through the day.

Now write the affirmation in your notebook and allow this positive statement about your potential to penetrate into your consciousness.

To program your right hemisphere, it is important that you *feel* as well as *think* that those words are true. There are many ways you could imagine the feeling of those words. I'll suggest one way, and after you work with the image, see if there is some other way, using another imaginative scenario, that you can create this affirmation for your right hemisphere.

Take a deep, relaxing breath and imagine that you're in a place of great stillness and safety and peace. Allow your head to roll forward. Concentrate on feelings of peace and of acceptance. Imagine that someone (it might even be the Muse or an angel) stands before you now and feel the sensation of warm, healing hands upon your head. Let those hands represent the touch of the One who willed abundant things for your life. The healing hands represent the Giving of Creative Power and the Renewal of Creative Awareness.

Stay with the fantasy and play with it in any way that seems right for you.

13

The Second Day

You are in the process of change and that change is occurring because of *your decision to allow it to happen*. These exercises are only the "means of transportation" that will carry you into the uncharted areas of your creative self. Remember that the credit for the discovery is yours alone; it is *your* talent that is being revealed and it is *your* commitment to this excursion that makes it possible. Try to think of the exercises not as some mysterious process, but only as a vehicle capable of taking you safely and quickly to an area of great personal resources.

As you begin your second day of right-brain experiences, remember the basic necessities: a quiet place where you can work without interruption; a block of time that is for you alone; a commitment that allows you to try new experiences with a spirit of expectation.

Settle into your favorite chair in your workroom. Before you begin the work today, turn to page 129 to the Awareness Chart and find the number that reflects what you are feeling now.

Close your eyes and give attention to the sounds around you. If there is silence, relax and enjoy it. If there are distracting sounds, know that your mind can block them out of your awareness; concentration creates its own kind of quiet.

CATEGORY 1.
OUTSMARTING THE LEFT BRAIN

Mandala # 2

The design of the mandalas will be different each day but they accomplish the same purpose. Remember the specific reasons why the mandala is used as an opening exercise. It will:

- center your attention
- quiet the chattering of your inner dialogue
- distract the left hemisphere, which cannot deal with spatial relationships
- allow the right hemisphere to dominate for an extended period of time

Focus directly on the center of the mandala on the next page and release your mind of all thoughts. Allow your right brain to deal with the spatial material.

CATEGORY 2.
BIOFEEDBACK TRAINING

Colors of the Mind

Be sure that you are in a comfortable position. Close your eyes. Check your breathing to be sure it is coming from deep within your chest. Exhale and then inhale to the count of five—pulling the air in through your nose until your lungs are full; hold for the count of five; exhale for the count of five.

Again, breathe in . . . and hold . . . and breathe out. Now begin to breathe naturally, finding your own rhythm.

Close your eyes and visualize the color red. Let it become as vivid a color as you can imagine.

> Imagine that color as a bright circle of red light above your head that covers your entire body with its glow. (If you have difficulty visualizing the color red, recall the apple in yesterday's exercise; transfer the color of that deep-red apple to the color of the light shining above you.)

Pretend that you can actually *breathe in* that color red.

Let it spread through your body, going into whatever parts of your body it wants to fill.

If any thoughts come in with the color, just let them come in and go right out again.

Thoughts will come to mind and move on—all your concentration is on the color that is moving slowly and easily through your body.

Visualize the color orange.

Picture it above your head, radiating a warm orange light.

Think of the color being drawn into your body

moving easily,
warm and soothing.
Let your body take whatever part of the color it needs.
Let the color go wherever it wants to go.
Allow whatever you don't need of this color to run out the bottom of your feet into the ground.

See a bright yellow light above your head.

Breathe in the light.
Let it go wherever it wants to go.
Let it warm you
and soothe you.
Whatever you don't want of it, let it run out the bottom of your feet.

See the color green above your head.

The green light moves through your body.
What you don't need runs through your body and out your feet into the ground.

Visualize the color blue above your head.

Pull the blue light into your body.
Let it comfort and soothe you.
What you don't need . . . release
through the bottom of your feet.

The purple light shines above you,

> breathe it in . . .
> feel the color moving gently through
> your body into the ground.

A bright, white light shines above you.

> Breathe deeply and pull it into
> your body until you are filled with
> brightness . . .

> feel it flowing through you, moving slowly,
> wonderfully soothing—
> and moving on . . .

Picture yourself running or dancing—

> easily, smoothly, beautifully . . .
> surround yourself with the light
> from any of the colors you experienced
> and be filled with the light . . .
> let the fantasy take you wherever it will . . .

When you are ready,

> slowly open your eyes and take time
> to enjoy the feeling. There is no need to rush.

When you feel that you're ready to move on to the next category of exercises, first take a moment to choose a number from the Awareness Chart (on p. 129) that reflects what you are feeling now.

CATEGORY 3.
GUIDED VISUALIZATION

A Place for You

Everyone needs a special kind of place, a retreat or sanctuary. A place that is safe and serene. In our real lives, most of us don't have a place that's exactly the way we want it to be. But we can give this to ourselves in fantasy.

If you could have the most wonderful place in which to work, where you could be creative and productive, I wonder what it would be like and where it would be located. Imagine for a moment that you can have this most wonderful place . . . this office or studio or workroom. It can be quite a spectacular place, if you like, for you aren't held to a budget. It can be built any way you want it to be built, on any piece of land, any place in the world.

Your imagination can give you everything you need and want. Think about the type of place it could be—in the city, or out in the country, perhaps in another country. It could have trees, or ocean, or mountains, or be a high-rise penthouse apartment in the middle of the city. You may be influenced by some inspirational place you have been or always wanted to go. Or you may prefer to envision something totally new and different.

Close your eyes; let your mind scan the earth as images drift into your awareness and move on. Don't be too quick to make a choice. You may want to entertain several possibilities as various thoughts and images come to your mind.

Get a sense of the kind of place that is right for you. When you find the area, imagine how the room is built. Be inside the house. Look around and notice the furniture and the appointments. Look at the colors, the textures. Are there any sounds? Any particular scent? Remember, you can have anything you want in this room. Make a list of things you see that are important to you; these will be a permanent part of this retreat.

Now make a list of the things that you want to keep *out* of this room. (You might consider the things that intrude upon your life in a normal day.) The items on this list need never intrude upon this special personal place that is yours alone.

In your fantasy, you can come back to this room as often as you want. You can stay as long as you want to be there. Right now, you might imagine going over to that chair that is so comfortable, that is just right for you, and know that this room belongs to you and the view outside the window is the view you want to see. Nothing can ever come into that room that is not right for you. No person can visit without an invitation. You can always go to that room in your imagination. It belongs only to you.

Open your eyes and take a deep breath. As you do, feel the creative energy that brings you oxygen and clarity and insights. Consider the uniqueness of the place you have created. And consider your own uniqueness when you are in that place.

Creating your special retreat may have given you an exhilarating feeling, stirring a strong need to begin work in that place that is yours only. Or it may have caused you to feel a quiet sureness that you have, in some inexplicable way, made contact with the special needs of your creative self. Whatever feelings are associated with this place are not to be dealt with lightly. You have taken a critical step in this program. Your Muse (or your angel, your intuitive self) has chosen a place to work.

Expect exciting and creative insights to emerge from that special workroom.

CATEGORY 4.
TRANSITIONAL OBJECTS

Wisdom From the Past

Look at the shoes you are now wearing. Then close your eyes and visualize those shoes in your mind's eye. Take that special kind of breath that will help you return to a state of deep relaxation. Think of a pair of shoes you had a year ago. Don't fight for the image, let it come easily or not at all. Let time roll back even further and imagine a pair of shoes you wore for a special occasion:
tennis shoes or dancing shoes or wedding shoes or . . .

Let the images move quickly before you.
You may think of school shoes . . .

The ones you wore in high school . . .
in grade school . . .
even before.

Let your imagination play with the memory until you finally stop searching—when you find the pair that you would like to use to experience going back to a distant time. These shoes will be the transitional objects that take you back to memories selected by your unconscious for this exercise.

*BE SURE THAT THE SHOES YOU HAVE CHOSEN WERE NOT
WORN DURING A TIME OF INTENSE TRAUMA.*

Put the shoes you have chosen on the floor of your fantasy.
Imagine that your feet are the size that they were when you
wore those shoes. Imagine your height, the shape of your body.

Put the shoes on and walk around until they feel comfortable on
your feet. Remember the way your body felt then . . . how tall you
seemed. . . . Remember the room where you dressed as a child. Look
around you; notice the things before you.

Look down at these shoes of your childhood;
if you are wearing socks, what color are they?

Walk out of the house and let your shoes direct your path. Follow
the familiar path to the sidewalk. Notice the colors around you, the
smell of the air.

When you come to a place where you should turn right or left,
turn in the direction that seems natural to you and keep walking. Let the shoes take you to the place in your memory that
your unconscious has in mind.

Keep your eyes closed until you are led into that memory and can
experience it fully. When you feel it is time, open your eyes and begin
to write: Where did the shoes take you? Who did you see? What did
you feel?

If the memory you experienced was a happy one, let the good
feelings from that experience be enriching for you again.

If the memories that surfaced are painful, there are ways you
can modify that memory. *You don't have to choose to harbor
the pain.* Go back again, even if the experience made you feel
sad or angry. Go back and *rework the script.*

Write new dialogue for the people to speak. Have the action change
to the way you wished it had been. Write a new ending and record it
in your notebook.

Before you return to your workroom and to the present, allow the
adult that you have become to comfort (to love, to help . . .) the child
that you were. Let the feelings of your inner child be consoled by the
accepting, caring nature of the adult part of yourself.

CATEGORY 5.
OTHER-HAND WRITING

Synthesizing Goals

Close your eyes and visualize a wild horse, or a herd of wild horses, racing across the beautiful mountain ranges of Montana or Wyoming. Watch the sense of freedom, of power and energy. In your mind's eye, *become* that wild creature. Feel the sensation of running with abandon, head tossing, wind pressing against you, traveling on.

> Remember how easy this was to do when you were a child? Remember how you ran with a stick or broom between your legs and made horse noises and tossed your head in the breeze? Well, didn't you?

Visualize a bird, which represents another form of freedom. Maybe it's an eagle, alone and powerful, climbing to heights beyond the highest mountain. Or a sea gull, playing over the ocean, swooping and climbing, soaring on the wind.

> In your mind's eye, become the bird.
> Feel the sense of freedom and the sensation of flying—the spreading of powerful wings and the joy of gliding.

Go with your own imagining; follow wherever it leads.
Be aware of the power and the energy . . . of the bird . . . of the horses. . . .

> Think of something you, in your real life, would like to do— something you wish you were free enough to do. Think of something you want that is not impossible but seemed just beyond your grasp.

Complete the next sentence and keep writing as the thoughts motivate you.
"What I really wish I could do now is . . ."
Take your pen in your non-dominant hand and, even though your writing will be difficult to read, begin to write with your "awkward hand." Don't stop to think, just write in your notebook. "What I really wish I could do is . . ."

It is possible that your left hand has stimulated additional awareness from your right hemisphere.

Before taking any action in the real world, consult your left hemisphere a few hours after you have finished these exercises. Remember, the right brain can give you invaluable insights into your feelings and suggest new possibilities to you in wonderful ways. However, it is not to be trusted until you have consulted your censor and logical critic at a time when it is more available for analyzing options.

If your two hands were in dramatic disagreement, use your notebook to reflect upon the conflict.

CATEGORY 6.
SENSORY STIMULATION

A Different Way of Seeing

It is quite an extraordinary experience to rediscover your world visually. You'll realize how little you usually "see" when you complete this exercise. Seeing with the observing eyes of a very young child makes the world new again; you find a miracle, not a mundane reality to be taken for granted.

Look around the room for a moment, observing not in words but in pictures. Try to see the room without giving things labels. When your eyes find a chair, observe its lines and curves and design; try very hard not to think: "chair, wooden arms, spot on cushion . . ." Instead, try to experience the chair with your eyes, notice the contours and textures and details.

Take five or ten minutes to rediscover the room. Do many awarenesses come to mind? Patterns of light?

Choose one of the things in the room that you particularly enjoy— the rose in the bud vase, the log beside the fire, a painting . . .

Rediscover that item as if for the first time. Observe it until you feel you know every curve, every subtle change of color. Without words, experience this thing that interests you. See the color without naming the color, observe the contours without using words in your mind.

Let your eyes find the wonder. Like a little child . . . enjoy.

Close your eyes. Observe the shifting patterns, the images that linger and fade.

What can you remember about the room as you sit with your eyes closed?

> With your eyes still closed, let your memory scan the room. Can you re-create the room in your mind's eye?

Is there some other room you would enjoy remembering? If you would like to re-experience some event in your past, begin by re-creating the place where it happened.

> If you want to remember what someone said, remember the colors in the room, the contours, the specific items within your vision.

Recall the sounds that were in the room, the smells, the feel of the textures touching your skin. If you were eating, can you find a memory of the taste?

> Now, can you remember the conversation? The people? Your response to the experience?

Write down in your notebook the memories and, with them, any imaginative additions you would like to make to your memory of the past.

Results From This
Right-Brain Experience

How might you use this new way of seeing to stimulate creativity in your everyday life? How could you transfer this interesting (but somewhat gossamer) visual experience into a tangible expression? Perhaps this story will give you some ideas for how visual intensity can effect your work.

Years ago, when I was in a fishing village in Alaska, I saw an old boat that lay wrecked upon the shore. Something about her fascinated me: the sense of abandonment, the sense of pride lost, the silent metaphor of mortality, perhaps.

Photography is an important matter in my life, and I spent the next half hour visually experiencing that ancient boat through various lenses. The telephoto lens intensified my awareness of the scars and gashes on the hull. The weather-stripped paint hung in curled ribbons, clutching the frame with only a fragile hold on the raw, exposed wood. A wider lens allowed me to envision the relationship of the boat to its surroundings. As she lay stuck there on the shore, another boat passed behind her in the inland passageway heading north. The contrast between the boats provided a different picture—and a shift in the philosophical direction my thoughts had taken.

This incident in "seeing intensely" became the catalyst for an important decision in my life. I realized that I had to *make* the time to use my talents.

The boat and the associations it conjured up imprinted a message on my right hemisphere that was, of course, perfectly obvious to my logical left brain: Dilettantes play with their creativity; professionals make it a priority. Not until that message engulfed my feeling self as well as my thinking self did the desire for a career become a reality.

CATEGORY 7.
FANTASY

A Distant Place,
A Forward Time

With your eyes closed, take a breath and return to a state of deep relaxation. Let your mind wander forward to a time in the future. It could be a year from now, ten years or twenty. Imagine the age that you will be then. Notice the shape of your body, the style of your hair.

Observe the people around you . . . the place where you are working. . . .

You are a very successful person and the work you have done for so many years is well appreciated. Experience the feeling of success and confidence.

Walk around te room of your future. Notice the decor, the colors. Consider how you respond to this place.

Wander through different aspects of your day. Where do you go when you leave work?

Where do you live?

Do you live alone or does someone live with you?

Describe the place where you live. See its details and record them in your notebook.

If you had to give up something to attain this lifestyle, write in your notebook about the thing you gave up.

Was this success worth the price you had to pay to attain it?

CATEGORY 8.
DREAM WORK

Decoding the Message

Copy in your notebook a dream you remember from last night. As you write the dream again, try to feel the experience of reliving it. If you can do this, new associations and insights will probably come to you. When you finish, go back and give a title to your dream. The title you choose will often give you a clue to the message your right brain sent you in the night.

Now write your associations to the dream.

What else does that make you remember? Write whatever comes to mind about anything at all. . . . Let your unconscious mind direct your thoughts. . . . Let ideas fly like a ball on the roulette wheel, spinning about and landing in unpredictable ways.

Gestalt therapists say that you can learn from a dream by "taking the part" of each element in the dream. It may feel strange to you at first to take on the emotions of the less acceptable attitudes of certain characters. But all the elements of the dream, at some level, reflect a part of yourself that seeks expression. Go back over the characters in your dream and enact the dream from each of their points of view. Even the non-human elements of the dream can be personified. Take the part of each of the characters in turn and even imagine that you are the setting itself. (If this presents a problem, read ahead to Results from This Right-Brain Experience and see if the work of others helps you interpret your own dream symbols.)

Results From This
Right-Brain Experience

A woman who appeared to be in her early fifties shared this dream with a small group in Los Angeles.

Setting: In my dream, I am in the penthouse of a tall building in Hawaii. I look out the window at the ocean and see a huge tidal wave approaching. I see my dog beside me and hear him whimpering. I watch the wave grow to enormous proportions. I feel it crash against the building, hear the shattering of glass, and then I am thrown far away from the structure of the building. I try to make my way back but it seems impossible. I keep trying, knowing that someone is depending on me, but I don't know who it is. I get back to the building, which seems to be intact. I straighten the furniture and keep feeling that I didn't understand how it could have survived the tidal wave. Other people are there but I don't know who they are.

Association: I've been worried about financial problems for a long time now. I'm involved in a real-estate venture that could really pull me under. The recession hit at just the wrong time for me and I'm afraid everything will be destroyed. I think the dream means this:

Hawaii is a setting that represents things peaceful and idyllic. The tidal wave seems to be the financial disaster I fear may destroy everything I worked for. The building represents all the success I've built up over the years.

Be the characters: I am Hawaii, peaceful and lazy in the sun. I like to please people, to smile.

I am the building, it took years of effort to become what I am today.

I am the penthouse, high above the crowd. Successful.

I am the flood, demanding and destructive and powerful and angry.

I am the dog, helpless and self-pitying.

I am the unknown people, representing parts of myself I don't understand.

I am the woman who goes back to fix things, to take care of the problem.

I am the furniture—out of place, but I could be set right.

From her second association: I think the dream really means to reassure me that I will survive no matter what happens. I will somehow know what to do. I suppose the building surviving the flood indicates that, at the deepest level, I don't think we will be forced into bankruptcy. Things are not as devastating as they seem. I pity the dog and know that I sometimes waste good energy just sitting and whining about the problem. I want to be more like the woman who stays calm in the storm and has the courage to work things through. The dog is that helpless part of me that is vulnerable, that whines, and is incapable of action.

When the destruction comes, my unconscious mind apparently feels that I will survive.

Going back to the building takes courage and is hard to do. Somehow the building has either remained intact or has been restored.

There is work for me to do to make things right, but it is not as devastating as I had feared.

Working with the dream enabled her to gain strength from unconscious awarenesses. She felt that her anxieties about a financial disaster had usurped her creative energies. Her associations to the dream helped her to feel more in control of her emotions. As a result, she was more productive in her work and certainly more comfortable with an extremely difficult problem.

CATEGORY 9.
FREE ASSOCIATION

Morning Wisdom # 2

Set your timer again for ten minutes and let your thoughts race against the clock. Let your mind jump and turn and make unexpected connections. Imagine that the words are being written *through* you and that your only job is to record the words onto paper. Keep the words you write as a secret from yourself; don't read them back. Trust that they will be even more fascinating when you read them on the sixth day and learn how to find unconscious metaphors.

CATEGORY 10.
GIFTS FROM THE RIGHT BRAIN

Awareness Summary # 2

At the close of each day, it's helpful to take stock of what these exercises have led you to discover.

Record from the Awareness Chart (p. 129) the number that best indicates what you are feeling now.

Has your ability to visualize improved during these sessions? Did you notice different reactions to specific colors? Which colors seem most relaxing? Were there any that you refused to let in, or that you were not comfortable with in some way? Is there a specific color that attracted your attention, that seemed the most peaceful or pleasurable? What appeals to you about that color?

As you stood in your "childhood shoes" and remembered events from the past, were you aware of the place that those feelings have in your present life, even after all those years have passed?

Did you get in touch with your inner child? If so, what felt most significant to you about that meeting?

Are you aware of any gestalts or ideas that occurred to you since you began this program? Throughout the day and evening, try to stay receptive to some insights that may be trying to get through.

Consider your schedule for the rest of the day: Will you be in a safe, relaxed situation or will you be with people who are challenging or putting you on guard in any way? Decide whether it is best to continue in this vulnerable state of slightly altered consciousness. Remember there are times you really *need* to let the left hemisphere, with all its defenses, be in charge.

If the exercises have revealed great surprises and many valuable insights, you won't need encouragement to be consistent in your schedule for working with this book. You will be drawn to it like a magnet. But if you have not yet experienced any astonishing revelations, you may need to be reassured that almost everyone begins to feel the effect of the exercises after the third day. Be patient with yourself and with me. We will move at the rate your unconscious wishes. Neither your anxiousness nor my coaxing will allow anything to happen until your right hemisphere is ready.

CATEGORY 11.
AFFIRMATIONS

Appreciation

Every day, at the close of your work time, you can use an affirmation to reinforce your confidence and program both hemispheres to accept the gift of creativity.

A feeling of gratitude, of thankfulness—some people would even say, a spirit of praise—has a renewing effect upon both body and mind. An affirmation will focus the attention of both brain hemispheres upon the feeling of appreciation for your creative talents.

First program your left hemisphere with the following affirmation:

I,_____, feel grateful for my creative powers. You, _____, feel grateful for your creative powers. She (He), _____, feels grateful for her (his) creative powers.

Remember to write your name in each of the three blank spaces. Then read each line aloud as you write the three sentences in your notebook.

Say this affirmation to yourself five times over the next twenty-four hours, each time concentrating upon the feeling of gratitude. If you do so, you will begin to have even greater appreciation for your innate talents, and focusing your attention upon them will help you feel more confident.

To program your right brain, your feeling self, take a deep breath and, with eyes closed, create the following scene in your mind's eye:

Imagine that you are in the special retreat that you designed for yourself. Allow a sense of quiet and peace to fill your mind. Look at the palm of your hand; wiggle your fingers slowly, and as you do, be aware of what a wonderful miracle of life you are! Look at the power you have to work such wonders by thought alone. Only the most jaded of people can fail to marvel at the very wonder of one's own existence. Close your eyes now and hold both hands before you with palms lifted upward. Offer some feeling of appreciation to the Giver of Life and Creativity. Express that gratitude, not in words, but in feelings generated from the center of silence that is within you. (If this is uncomfortable for you, perhaps you would like to create some other way to help you appreciate the uniqueness of your existence and of your creativity.)

14

The Third Day

In a country far removed from Western civilization, an archaeologist discovered a drawing which indicated that a great treasure was buried in the interior regions of this distant land. The gems were located in a primitive area where stone and rock formations had made previous travel quite difficult. Motivated by the discovery of the map and aided by an unusual vehicle with greater capabilities than even a four-wheel–drive, the archaeologist set forth to uncover the secret wealth which had long existed in the interior of his country.

On this third day of our expedition into uncharted regions of your creative mind, you are much like the archaeologist in our story. You, too, have a map and a means of transportation. But finding the buried wealth depends not only upon these aids, but upon your willingness to move into unfamiliar terrain, to encounter whatever creatures dwell in the area, and to dig into bedrock to release one of the greatest treasures of all: the power of creativity.

Your journey begins in the security of your workroom. Is the phone unplugged? Are pets outside? (Would a DO NOT DISTURB sign hanging on the outside of your door be helpful?)

Begin your work by assessing your level of feeling. Turn to p. 129 and find the number that reflects what you are feeling now.

Each day you will probably find it a little easier to assess your creative energy. Becoming attuned to this feeling will be extremely helpful as you begin to take charge of your creative powers. If you still find this assessment difficult, don't allow frustration to build. Relax with the question and allow the answer to surface whenever it will.

CATEGORY 1.
OUTSMARTING THE LEFT BRAIN

Mandala # 3

You are no doubt growing more accustomed to the use of the mandala as, each day, a new drawing is presented to you. Perhaps you are finding out that each time you can enjoy using the mandala for a longer period of time. Each of the designs is going to offer you a slightly different experience. By the time you have worked with all six of them, you will probably have chosen the one or two that are the most pleasing to you.

In my seminars, I find that people tend to have strong feelings about which mandala is best for them. This is a highly subjective matter and you will undoubtedly form your own choices as the work progresses.

Remember to focus only on the center of the design and allow your peripheral vision to play with the pattern. Relax and enjoy the experience; avoid any temptation to analyze the design. Allow your spatially expert right hemisphere to work in its own way, without interference.

CATEGORY 2.
BIOFEEDBACK TRAINING

Imagining

Consider how you are feeling now.

Is your body tense or relaxed?
Is your mind anxious or calm?
Be aware of the relationship between your body and your mind.

During this exercise, you will become more relaxed and peaceful. Be sure you are in the most comfortable place in the room. Your clothing should be loose. Let your legs stretch out before you and your arms lie easily beside your body. Close your eyes.

Without changing its pattern, notice your breathing.

Remember yesterday's exercise and how relaxing it was to take full, deep breaths?

Put your hand over your diaphragm as you inhale through your nose.

One . . . two . . . three . . . four . . . five

Feel the air pushing your hand higher and higher and higher.

Think of a balloon expanding
one . . . two . . . three . . . four . . . five

And release the air through your mouth—

As if you are blowing an imaginary
feather into the air.
And slowly count to five.

Take another deep breath.

One . . . two . . . three . . . four . . . five
hold . . . two . . . three . . . four . . . five . . .
let it out through your mouth . . . four . . . five

Begin scanning your body for tension—start with your feet and wiggle your toes.

Imagine the tension falling away
as you tighten
and hold . . .
and relax

Feel the relaxation in your ankles as you rotate them.

As all of the tension falls away,
as all the strain slips away

Concentrate on your calves as you

tighten . . .
hold . . .
relax . . .

And on your thighs as you

tighten . . .
hold . . .
relax . . .

Then your buttocks as you

> tighten . . .
> hold . . .
> relax . . .

Concentrate on your abdomen

> tighten . . .
> hold . . .
> relax . . .

All of your shoulder muscles . . .
All of your back muscles . . .
Now your arm muscles . . .
Now your fingers, as you make a fist

Rotate your neck . . . very slowly . . .

Feel the tension cracking and breaking away.

If there are any areas of your body that are still tense, that need to be stretched,

> stretch them now.

If there is any tension left in your body, think of it as a liquid that flows into the heel of your left foot.

> Very slowly now, let all of that tension drain from your heel into the floor. Imagine that you can feel that last residue of tension moving through your heel and disappearing as if gravity itself had pulled it away from you.

Scan your body with your thoughts and be aware of how relaxed you feel now.

> Feel the relaxation in your legs.
> And in your pelvic area.
> Consider your upper torso.

> > Your arms . . .
> > your shoulders . . .
> > your neck.

Notice the stillness of your spirit.

Be thankful for the peaceful feelings.

Be aware that your right hemisphere has been getting stronger and more confident.

How do you feel now? Refer the Awareness Chart (p. 129)

CATEGORY 3.
GUIDED VISUALIZATION

Getting Rid of the Problem

Take one of those smooth, relaxing breaths that start deep in the center of your being and is drawn into your lungs and then blown slowly through your lips into the air.

> And once again . . .
> And one more time.

Imagine that you are on an island in the South Pacific on a beach where the sand is fine and white and clean. The ocean is warm and gentle in the cove where you have come to spend part of this day. Listen to the easy rhythm of the waves.

> This is a calm and private place; the silence is broken only by ocean sounds. You are safe here. It is a place of peace and of healing. Lie down in the sand and enjoy the feeling of deep relaxation.

Enjoy the softness of the sand that is dry and molded around your body. Be conscious of the warmth of the air and the sand pressing against your body, from the heels of your feet that press into the powdery softness of the sand through all parts of your body to the very top of your head.

Is there something in your life you would like to get rid of?

> A physical pain or illness?
> an emotion that is destructive?
> an anxiety that disturbs you?

Using the first image that comes to your mind, give the thing you want to be rid of, *some physical shape.*

It could be round like a ball . . .
square like a steel cabinet . . .
linear like a piece of string.

Can you see the shape of this thing?

Feel the weight of it . . .
Notice the color . . .
What is the texture?
Does it have an odor?

Place all of your concentration on the thing until you know every contour of it, every inch of its form. Visualize it so clearly in your mind's eye that there are no hidden parts. Now imagine that it is small enough to fit in the palm of your hand.

Take this thing and put it in your right hand or your left hand.

Be aware that if it is in your hand, it is no longer in your body . . . it is no longer a part of you. The thing you want to be rid of is in the palm of your hand.

Place this thing about a foot away from you on the sand. When you are ready, slowly sit up and feel the sand shift beneath you as your weight changes.

Look at the thing you want to be rid of and carefully observe its size.

Dig a hole in the sand that is considerably larger than the thing itself. Notice how the sand moves easily, for it is dry and of fine texture and it responds quickly to the movement of your hands.

Take as long as you need to dig the hole that is wider and deeper than the thing you will be rid of.

When you are ready, take the thing in both of your hands; drop it or push it into the hole.

If you find that the hole is not deep enough, or wide enough, take the time to make it right. You can remove the thing if you need to dig the hole larger. Be sure the hole is much deeper than you actually need.

When you feel this thing you want to be rid of is placed properly and deeply into the hole, you can begin to cover it with sand.

Using your hands, push the sand into the hole. Then use your arms and scoop the sand around and cover the thing, filling the hole until it exists no more and the surface of the area is flat.

Now smooth the sand until even the traces of your fingertips disappear.

Look carefully at the smooth sand and know that the thing you would be rid of is beneath the sand, that it has been buried with great ritual.

Now stand up and move away from the burial place and turn your back on it.

Look and see how the tide has moved closer and is now gently lapping at your feet. Watch how slowly each wave approaches.

Welcome it to your body . . .
feel the warm water move up your legs . . .
white foam, frothing around you . . .
ocean sounds . . .
like the sea's laughter . . .

And the next wave moves up to your waist and you feel like a child again, playing in a safe place, knowing, trusting that everything will be fine and there is no harm that will come to you.

You may walk further into the sea if you enjoy the feeling. Or you may return to the shore and let the sun dry your body. Choose which is best for you . . . and delight in the feeling.

When you are finished, take a very deep breath and know, as this exercise is finished, that the thing you want to be rid of is buried deeply in the sand on an island far away. Open your eyes and be aware of your presence in your own place. Be aware of how far away this place is from that distant island.

The thing that used to be a part of you is a part of you no more.
Write about this experience in your notebook in as much detail as possible. What did you choose to be rid of? What shape did you give it? What experience did you have when you buried it?

Results From This
Right-Brain Experience

A woman who feared speaking in public was preparing to do so several days after one of my workshops.

When she buried her speaking anxiety—which was shaped like a round steel ball with sharp protrusions around its surface (which reminded me of a medieval weapon)—it was so powerful it exploded from the hole! She grabbed it and stabbed it with a weapon that pierced the steel, and the anxiety deflated as easily as a rubber ball. Then she dropped it into the hole and watched it flop around like a dying fish. When the thing finally died, she covered the hole and walked away from it.

Later, she told me her speech was well received. More important perhaps was the fact that she gained some ability to separate herself from the intensity of her fears.

CATEGORY 4.
TRANSITIONAL OBJECTS

Re-creating Success

Close your eyes and take a deep relaxing breath, and then another. Clear your mind of internal chatter. Release any tension in your body. When you feel the inner stillness, you are ready to begin.

Imagine that you are walking over a wooden bridge to a place you vaguely remember being in many years ago. Walk around for a while until you find a particular place you like and sit down. Let the light be dim in the place you have chosen and let the place you are sitting be comfortable. In this place you are secure and safe.

> Imagine that there is a voice speaking the number that is your age; and listen as the quiet, friendly voice counts backwards, a year at a time, while good memories come into awareness as the years roll backwards in your mind.

When you come to a year that holds a particularly wonderful memory associated with a feeling of success and general well-being, stop at that year.

Perhaps there is a specific event that has caught your attention. Or maybe it is only a general sensation of contentment. Allow yourself to thoroughly experience that feeling and let it carry you where it wants you to go.

If parts of the memory are diffused by time, you will be able to remember the experience better if you think first of the colors that you associate with that situation. Does a specific color come to mind? What is the color?

Are there sounds that you can hear in your memory? Take time to listen to the sounds. Identify any sounds that creep around the edges of your memory.

Can you remember any specific odors?

If the textures of your clothing or of a blanket or a person's touch come to mind, stay with the feeling.

Are there tastes that you recall?

If you want the memory to come back to you, welcome it to your mind. You can choose to dis-remember any unpleasantness and recapture only the nurturing parts of the experience. In the work that we are doing, it is not the reality of the event but the quality of the experience that is important to recall.

Stay with the good feelings that remind you of that nurturing time. Let the blending of memory and fantasy carry you into a feeling of satisfaction and confidence.

Keep your eyes closed as you experience the memory. Then, when you are ready to open your eyes, write down in your notebook everything that you remember right away. Record your feelings and observations, the colors and sounds and tastes and textures.

As you move away from this experience, keep the good feelings with you and let any memory of sadness pass away from you. Retain only that which is good for you to recall. Write a list of the nourishing things you choose to remember from your childhood. Make a list of the things you choose to move beyond and leave behind.

CATEGORY 5.
OTHER-HAND WRITING

Suspending Judgement

Suspending judgement while you evaluate many options is an effective tool for problem-solving. This will help you to avoid making a quick decision and allow you to seek out better solutions. Consider a problem that has troubled you and for which you have found no solution. This problem could be an "outside" problem, such as whether to change jobs, or an "inside" problem, such as loneliness. Write the problem as clearly and specifically as you can.

Since you have been aware of this problem, you have probably tried—or thought of trying—some specific solutions. There were probably some solutions you dismissed because your "logical mind" told you the solution wasn't viable. Make a list of the things you tried or wanted to try, and then a list of the things you thought of trying but rejected.

It is probable that some other solutions have been trying to emerge from your creative unconscious, but have been held back for a variety of reasons. Perhaps your "critic" has jumped to harsh conclusions and rejected certain ideas too soon. Perhaps the suggestions from your unconscious cannot be heard over the sound of pre-determined judgement.

In your mind's eye, imagine what your critic looks like—the one who pronounces these judgements. Surely, it is a stern character, terrified of failure and ridicule, fearful even of appearing silly or frivolous. Undoubtedly, this critic has appeared on the scene from time to time in the course of this program to admonish you for investing valuable time in "childish games." (Your high-minded critic may have even harsher terms.) Now get one precise picture of this critic. If possible, visualize your critic as a small creature; this exercise is *much* easier to do if you're dealing with a small creature. Now lift it in the air and carry it over to the ladder which is there on your right. This ladder is resting safely on a cross-beam in the center of the room. Climb the ladder, holding your critic carefully as you go, *and put it on top* of the chandelier. The chandelier is made of wrought iron and will neither swing nor break; it will suffice as a temporary "jail" for your awesome critic.

Now come down and move the ladder away from the chandelier. Come back to your original problem. Your critic cannot hear your thoughts from the high perch and therefore will make no comment. Reconsider your problem and list all of the other options that come to mind now. It doesn't matter if they sound silly or if you think someone might object or if there is some inherent problem down the line. List all of the options that come to mind; even those you think you'd never use.

Now, go back over these options again. Play with each one, hold it lightly in your mind, consider . . . consider . . . Does it make you think of something else? Does something make you wonder . . . what if . . . ?

Now take your pen in your non-dominant hand and make some notes. Write the ideas that come to you. Any thoughts whatever should be welcomed. Keep in mind that your unconscious mind may be sending you a special delivery message, even as you sit here. Be sure you keep the door of receptivity open during this time.

Later today, you will want to take your critic off the chandelier so that it can function properly. (Never *act* on right-hemisphere advice without left-hemisphere consultation!) But for now, just enjoy the freedom to imagine anything at all.

CATEGORY 6.
SENSORY STIMULATION

A Different Way of Hearing

Listen intently to the sounds that are in your room or working space.

Be aware of the silences between the sounds.

Notice the sounds outside your room.

And the silences between those sounds.

If there is noise outside your room, listen carefully to the rhythm of the sound. In your mind, amplify the sound by giving it intense concentration.

> Now, shut the sound out of your awareness. Create an imaginary, invisible "wall of silence" by concentrating on something else with great intensity. You can let the external sounds bounce off your imaginary wall.

If that is difficult for you to do, try listening to a sound of your own mental creation—perhaps a droning sound or a repetitive sound. Have you ever listened to a train *carefully*? There is something wonderous about the sound of it. (Ask any child, if you have forgotten.)

> Close your eyes, pretend that it is night in the country and you are standing a safe distance from the railroad tracks. Can you hear the warning bells from the junction a half mile away?

Can you hear the train far in the distance?

> Listen, as it comes closer . . . as the engine passes in front of you . . . as each car clangs and rumbles beside you . . . Listen to each car and make the train as long or as short as you wish.

Listen as the caboose passes by. Be aware of how quickly the sound dies away after the passing, as if the sound falls off the edge of the earth.

> The train is gone and in the distance a dog howls at the moon.
> Can you hear the dog?
> And the silences?
> Are there crickets?

Return to the room you are in now.
What sounds do you hear in your workroom?

> If there were sounds before, are they still there?
> Did you hear them when the train was passing through your mind?

If you hear the sounds now but didn't hear them when you were busy *listening* to the train, you have experienced the power of your mind over external noise. This is a fine tool to have at your disposal for doing creative work. For, in a world of noise and confusion, you can create your own sounds—and your own silences. You can choose what to hear.

If your problem is how to sleep when people or dogs or cars are keeping you awake, you can solve that problem by creating alternative sounds in your mind.

If your problem is how to concentrate on your work when the world around you is polluting the air with noise, create your own silence inside your head.

If you want an unusual experience in sound, put your ear to the dishwasher and listen through the changing cycles. Let your imagination play any game it chooses.

Try to avoid having to explain to anyone what you are doing; taken out of context, this exercise can make you appear a tad peculiar!

CATEGORY 7.
FANTASY

Your Flying Machine

Take a deep relaxing breath and concentrate on your breathing. Imagine a place that is out of doors, that is relaxing and beautiful, and use your imagination to put yourself in that place. Lie down and feel the textures of the grass . . . or the sand . . . or whatever texture you choose.

Imagine the season of the year.

Imagine the hour of the day.

Imagine the temperature of the air and the feel of the air against your skin.

Let yourself feel calm and centered.

Imagine that your body is relaxed as it presses heavily upon the surface beneath you. Let your body feel heavier and heavier and more and more relaxed.

Now let the weight of your body feel like its normal weight; and then even lighter than usual, so very much lighter than usual. You feel so light it seems that you are resting very lightly on the surface beneath you. Think of the sensation of floating . . . or of lying on a warm waterbed.

Feel the warmth of the waterbed beneath you. Let it become a magic carpet that carefully and safely drifts a few feet above the earth.

Imagine what it would be like if you were able to fly.

What if people could fly as easily as they could swim under water? What if you could just move your arms and lift off into space?

You may want to float only a few feet above the earth at first. But when you're more confident of your power, you may choose to fly higher. If you would prefer to fly with some type of conveyance to aid you then, by all means, create one for your reassurance.

You might want to fly in a hot air balloon.

Or you might prefer to imagine great wings, like those used for hang-gliding.

You can create a wonderful contraption of your own design to help you fly.

If you're feeling cautious, put a parachute on your back.

Even though you know it's not really possible to fly unassisted . . . like most creative people, you know that you can experience the sensation of flying as clearly as if you had been born with wings.

Choose the way that you will fly.

Now lift into the air, going as high as you want to go and no higher.

You may want to go a few feet off the ground . . . or even into the cosmos to play at the edge of friendly stars.

You can go anywhere you want to go on earth or in the heavens.

You have the power to change the year . . .
move across great distances . . .
to go into the past or the future . . .

Fly as long as you want to, and when you choose, come down into any setting in heaven or on earth.

Someone is waiting for you there.
Someone from the present . . .
or the past . . . or the future.

Who is the person?

What does the person say?

How do you respond?

Write as much of this flying experience as you want to record in your notebook.

Results From This
Right-Brain Experience

A forty-six-year-old writer from California reported this fantasy:

"At first I wasn't comfortable with the idea of flying. I was afraid of losing control. I decided to only go a few inches off the ground—just enough to experience that "weightless" feeling. Then the waterbed became a rubber life raft and I felt like I was floating on the sea; and then the raft became a boat that could fly. I went up in the air a little ways, but when I wanted to look down at the earth, I was afraid I would fall out of the boat. So I changed the boat into a hang-glider so that I could sit up and see not only the heavens but the shore. I let the hang-glider carry me way up into space, lifting me higher and higher, and the world seemed small like in pictures from outer space. I realized then that I didn't need my glider anymore, so I flew off and left it floating there.

I played around the edge of a star—not a real star, but the child's kind with five points—and then I remembered this story of *The Little Prince* from my childhood and I wanted to visit him on his planet. I wanted to see his rose, which was such a matter of consequence. When I found the planet, the Prince wasn't home, but the rose told me he would be there another day if I wanted to come back. I flew higher and the air turned cold and I was torn between wanting to explore the high regions of outer space or return to a warmer level. I decided to come home because it was dark and I felt very much alone up there. So I flew down into the warmer air where it was daylight instead of dark. I saw a rainbow with the brightest colors I'd ever seen. It was shaped like a long roller coaster that descended all the way to earth.

I rode down the roller coaster all the way down past the stars and slipped back to earth.

It felt like a wonderful dream, and I'm glad I let myself have the experience.

CATEGORY 8.
DREAM WORK

What Aborigines Know

This experience is an adaptation of the techniques used by the Senoi tribe to gain power over terrifying dream figures. As I mentioned earlier, the Senoi learn to program their responses to dreams. Similarly, by working with dream figures in a state of deep relaxation, we can gain some control over negative dream symbols and their influence on our emotions.

Can you recall a dream in which you were a victim? Think of a time when you were the person being chased, or hurt, or terrified by someone or something. The Senoi would have you program your dream so that you wouldn't run away when you encountered trouble. They would say you should face it and fight. You could even enlist other dream characters to help you fight the dream enemies. Through this confrontation, it is possible to gain power over the negative part of yourself that created that dream terror. If you can remember such a dream, report it in your notebook.

Now go into that dream again. Experience it fully. Let your fear return as you face your enemies. Envision the set in your dream theater, retrace your steps and your feelings. But this time, turn and confront your attacker; call anyone you need to help you; fight until the harmful character is destroyed or conquered. Can you feel the sense of victory over the dream character? Write the feelings that surface as you gain control of a situation that has seemed horrifying in the past.

Demand that the defeated dream character give you a gift. It could be a poem or a song, an insight, or something that is useful in a tangible way. Take something useful back from the encounter. Write what you were given. Do you like it? Need it? Want it? If you dislike the gift, go back into the dream and demand a different gift. One can be rude and assertive with dream characters. It is not bad manners to dominate in dreams.

Can you recall a dream in which you had the sensation of falling? If so, write the dream in your notebook.

Now go back into the dream and try to experience again the

sensation of falling. But now you will have control over the fall. You can choose to fly; just pull out *easily* from the fall and level off. Feel the sensation of floating on the air, moving slowly, laterally, then soaring high into space. If for some reason you don't want to fly, then open a parachute and very carefully and slowly descend into a haystack and enjoy the trip. The Senoi would suggest you continue the fall, land gently, and see what surprises await you. They believe you have been called to a strange land by a part of yourself that is not often heard. There is a message for you there, something to learn or understand intuitively. Explore the new land. See if you can discover the insights that await you there.

CATEGORY 9.
FREE ASSOCIATION

Morning Wisdom # 3

Set your timer for ten minutes. Let your thoughts flow wherever they want to go. The logical sequential patterns of your left brain are useless in this exercise. Allow the rambling patterns of your right brain to draw upon unconscious feelings and associations. Remember not to read what you have written until you receive the directions for interpretation on the sixth day.

CATEGORY 10.
GIFTS FROM THE RIGHT BRAIN

Awareness Summary # 3

Note down from the Awareness Chart (on p. 129) the number that best indicates what you are feeling now. You may find that you are able to define your feelings much more quickly than you were before starting these exercises.

While using the mandala, have you begun to actually feel the change in your brain waves? Some people notice it during their first days in the program. Others never become aware of a physiological change, but can tell they are working in the right-brain mode because of sudden flushes of unconscious material.

Consider the thing you wanted to be rid of. Does the shape or texture you chose for its form give you any indication of your feeling about the thing? Were you able to distance yourself from its power when you buried it? Is there anything in the nature of your right brain's attitude that your left brain needs to understand? If so, write about it in your notebook.

When you suspended judgement for a while, were you aware of how many ideas seemed to float to the surface? Can you see how effective your right brain can be when it has a chance to play freely with ideas?

What did you learn from your flying experience? Did you observe the world from a new perspective? If so, did that observation change any specific concept you have about your present situation?

Was anything frightening or unpleasant during your fantasy time? If so, it may be helpful to pay attention to those signals from your unconscious; these are areas of potential trouble for you. If the feelings were not extremely painful, you will benefit from evaluating them and trying to understand why they have power over you. If you experienced negative feelings, express them and record your observations about them.

There has been great stimulation of your imaginative hemisphere; try to remain receptive to any new idea or feeling that may emerge in the hours between now and your next session in the workroom. Be sensitive to your schedule, however, and remember not to place yourself in an emotionally threatening situation while you are still vulnerable.

CATEGORY 11.
AFFIRMATIONS

Using the Gift

Like the archaeologist in the story I told earlier, you have set out to find something of great value. You have at last found the place where the treasure lies; now it is yours for the taking.

Even the finest valuables bring no pleasure if they stay hidden away forever; they need to be seen and they need to be used and enjoyed. Creative potential longs for expression. Remember the words of Robert Kirsch: "May I love my work and the doing of it."

The Affirmation for the third day of the program will encourage you to use that unique creativity which only you can express.

Put your name in the blank space on each line in the affirmation below, which you copy into your notebook. As you say each line aloud and write each line in the space provided, remember the association you can call forth to strengthen the effect of these words. For example, when you say,

"I,_____, have a strong desire to express my creativity in all of its forms," you know that is a mature attitude which will help you to stay motivated.

When you say, "You,_____, have a strong desire to express your creativity in all of its forms," you can imagine someone close to you encouraging you with those words.

When you say, "She (He)_____ has a strong desire to express her (his) creativity in all of its forms," you might imagine a person whose imagination and commitment you greatly admire and visualize that person affirming your motivation.

Now write down the three affirmation sentences and use those associations to your best advantage.

To program your right brain, you will benefit from finding a non-verbal way to experience that motivation. Begin in the traditional way, with eyes closed and a deep breath taking you into a state of relaxation. Focus on a place connected with an area of creativity in which you would like to express yourself. It might be an artist's studio, a concert hall, a drafting table, or any place in your home or office where creative activities would increase your pleasure. Visualize yourself in that place. Imagine that you are working at the very thing you want to do. See yourself doing a fine job, experience the feeling of achievement—not through words, but through that inner awareness that feels so wonderful. Experience your work and the doing of it. Take joy in the work—in the process of its development. Success is not only defined by the praise and reward from others, it is first defined in your own awareness and consciousness. Give yourself the satisfaction of knowing that the work you are doing in this visualization is fine work and that you can take pride in your efforts and your achievement.

15

The Fourth Day

During the first few days of a vacation, if you travel to a place where you have never been before, you may experience a certain anxiety along with the pleasure. After all, new places and new experiences are associated with the mysterious "unknown." But by the fourth day you have probably settled into your new environment and, if the location of your trip has been favorable, you have begun to relax and thoroughly enjoy the adventure.

In this interior journey, initially you may have felt some of those same kinds of anxieties. You may have wondered whether the exercises would arouse more feelings than you cared to deal with. Would the stimulation provide the results you expected? Would the promises made in the beginning of the book be fulfilled?

Now, at the beginning of the fourth day, I hope you have caught the excitement that most people feel in this program. Let these exercises provide the vehicle that leads you into new encounters with your inner self. Remember that an integration of the past with the present enables you to draw from all of your experiences for your creative work.

Be sure that you are in a comfortable position and that you have provided for privacy during your work time. As on every day of this program, it is important to evaluate your feelings of tension or relaxation before you begin. Mark the number from the Awareness Chart (on p. 129) that will help you describe what you are feeling at this very moment.

Now focus your attention on the chart at the point of deep relaxation. Imagine what that state of silence and inner peace will feel like as you approach it today.

CATEGORY 1.
OUTSMARTING THE LEFT BRAIN

Mandala # 4

When you focus on the mandala on the next page, be conscious of your ability to experience "centering." You do this activity without words, without thoughts, with only your right brain's way of knowing. You will begin to feel that concerns from your ordinary reality will not penetrate the concentration you attain by using the mandala. The inner chatter of your left-hemisphere thinking will fade into a whisper and then into silence.

CATEGORY 2.
BIOFEEDBACK TRAINING

A Matter of Suggestion

As you sit in your most comfortable chair, attune your mind to your body and consider the message it is sending to you. Then consider your emotions and be aware of the relationship between your mind and your body.

Take a deep breath, the kind you have learned that is easy and restful. Use the count of five as your rhythm as you inhale . . . and hold . . . and exhale again.

Take another deep breath—
perhaps one more.

Let all of your concentration be on your feet and on any areas of tension in them. Breathe naturally, and as you inhale, imagine that you are drawing all the tension from your feet up through your body into your lungs. Hold the mental image of that tension. And now, slowly, imagine that you are exhaling all of that tension out through your mouth. You will feel as if you are literally blowing away the tension, exhaling all the destructive tightness out of your body.

> Allow the tension from your feet
> to be gone and . . . relax.

Concentrate on the tension in your legs. As you inhale, imagine that you are pulling all the tension from your legs into your lungs. Hold the tension for the count of five . . . and imagine that you are exhaling all of that tension out of your body into the air.

> Allow the tension from your legs to be gone and . . . relax.

Concentrate on the tension in your buttocks, then all around the abdomen and pelvic area. Draw all of the tension out of the area as you inhale and pull the tension into your lungs. Hold the tension; slowly blow the tension away from your body.

> Allow the tension from your buttocks and abdomen and pelvic
> area to be gone.
> And relax.

And now your chest and shoulders. Draw the tension into your lungs and release it through your mouth as you exhale.

> Allow the tension from your chest and shoulders to be gone
> and . . . relax.

Then your arms, as you draw that tension up into your lungs. Holding it . . . two . . . three . . . four . . . five and blowing it out of your mouth, out of your body, into the air.

> Allow the tension from your arms to be gone and . . . relax.

Feel the tension in your neck. Draw that tension into your lungs and hold it, releasing it as you blow it away.

> Allow the tension from your neck to be gone and . . . relax.

The tension in your head moves into your lungs as you breathe and then is blown out of your body as you exhale.

> Allow the tension from your head to be gone and . . . relax.

The left side of your brain is not at all interested in what you have just been doing.

> Your right brain is stimulated now and is ready to help you
> reach your goals.

Enjoy the feeling of peace and confidence. Take a moment to consider the changes that are beginning to happen as your right brain takes charge. Can you feel the shift from left hemisphere to right?

Be aware of the changes in your mind and body. Note the appropriate number from the Awareness Chart (on p. 129).

CATEGORY 3.
GUIDED VISUALIZATION

The Secret Cave

Begin your visualization with a deep relaxing breath and return to the woods you entered on the first day of the program. Let the air be cool against your skin and the day wrapped in fog.

> When you enter the woods, be aware of the sounds you hear . . . and the smell of the forest . . . and the mood of the forest. . . .

Walk to the stream and watch the rushing water for a moment. Enjoy its sounds and observe how it breaks against the rocks before you find a safe place to cross to the other side.

> Now take a new path, one that leads to the mountain trail. Follow the trail that leads you higher into the mountains . . . and higher . . . until your legs feel the strain . . . until you don't want to climb anymore.

> Stop and look around you. Find the cave that is almost hidden by the rocks. Know that you will not be harmed inside the cave and that you will find something of great importance there.

> As you walk into the cave, the air feels cool against your skin. Wait a moment; let your eyes grow accustomed to the dim light. The walls of the cave are rough and damp. Reach out and feel the dampness. Notice the sound of a distant waterfall somewhere deep within the cave.

> There is a soft, golden light coming from a high opening; you can see into the next room-like cavern. Walk into the next room and explore the cave.

As you move into a still deeper part of the cave, a fire glows from one side of the cavern and you can see that someone is seated beside it on a large, flat rock. You have encountered someone with great wisdom and insight, someone who can reveal to you the answer to important questions, and whom you have every reason to trust. This person has known about you for a very long time.

Ask this very special person any question that is important to you. Note down the question that you asked.

What is the answer you received?

Be aware that this wise and caring person was created by the powers of your right brain—just for the purpose of helping you understand the more secret parts of yourself.

Let your imagination keep you in this cave a little longer. In the next exercise, you will explore its inner passages and discover wonderful surprises.

CATEGORY 4.
TRANSITIONAL OBJECTS

Cave Drawings

You are still in the inner room of the cave with the wisest, most caring person that you can imagine. The questions you asked of this special person have been answered and it is time for you to explore even deeper regions of this cave. There is nothing here that will be harmful to you and the discoveries you make will enrich your understanding of yourself.

Follow this wise person into the next chamber. There you find a large oval room where the walls are smooth and soft sand lies beneath your feet. A narrow channel of water runs through the room. The water is four-feet deep and, at its widest point, the water spreads to a width of twelve feet.

A boat waits for you in the water; it is small and securely built. The loving person helps you onto the boat for a journey that will take you to a place of vivid memories. There may be something you want to say to this person before you leave; if so, take a moment to write it in your notebook.

And what is it that you perhaps felt but did not bring yourself to say?

What does this person say to you before you go?

Was there anything that you wished had been said to you that was not said? If so, write what you wanted to hear.

And listen while this caring person says those words to you now.

If you have great difficulty saying goodbye, you can ask this wise and loving person to go with you on your journey.

> The boat is powered in a unique way: it moves forward or backward as you direct it with your thoughts. When you are comfortably settled in the boat, direct the boat forward and notice how easily it moves through the water—slowly and safely. . . . The automatic pilot guides your boat through the water while you watch the changing scene around you.

Notice that there are frescoes on the walls of the cave. These paintings are a vast mural depicting times in your life when you felt good about yourself and the decisions you were making. They show how capable and talented you really are.

> Direct your thoughts to pull the boat close to the edge of the water so you can look more closely at the pictures. Notice how confident and happy you seem in the drawings. Some of the pictures show "small moments," intimate times with a friend. Other drawings recall more public experiences.

Write in your notebook what you see in the paintings on the walls.

When you are ready, direct the boat forward and drift down the narrow river, watching scenes from earlier years until you find one that particularly appeals to you. Write what you see.

Direct the boat to stop and wait for you while you step onto the shore and walk to the wall of the cave to observe the scene more carefully.

Imagine yourself walking right into that scene, becoming one of the characters, the *central* character. As you step into the picture, it will carry you backwards into that time and that place, and your memory will recall everything that you want to remember about that time of your life.

Relive all that was good and nourishing about that time and release any disturbing feelings if they should arise. Relive the feelings of success. And now describe in writing what you feel and what you see.

Carry that feeling of success with you as you step back into the boat. Direct the boat to take you through the cavern, where you see scenery more beautiful than you have ever seen before. Let the river carry you all the way to the place of departure, into the sunlight, to a familiar place where you step onto the shore. Now, by the power of your thoughts, send yourself back into your work room.

CATEGORY 5.
OTHER-HAND WRITING

Intrusive Thoughts

Have you ever tried to get rid of certain thoughts that keep coming back against your will? They invade quiet moments, intrude upon your work, and create turmoil and anxiety. This exercise will show you how to get rid of those intrusive thoughts—if you really go deeply into this fantasy and allow it to become more real than the most vivid dream.

Two types of exercises are suggested here: one is for banishing hostile intruders, the other is for temporarily displacing friendly intruders. Both types can interfere with productivity and occasionally need to be put outside of your thoughts.

This visualization came to me one day while I was working on this book. Two quarrelsome people kept nagging at my imagination while I was trying to write. These people were neither family nor friends. Nonetheless, they seemed to have gained a great deal of power over my concentration. So I had to devise an exercise to get rid of them. These people, with their negative attitudes, had ruined hours of valuable work time before I discovered an effective way to evict them from my thoughts.

If you should happen to have a couple of haranguing people in mind—or even a couple of anxieties that disturb your concentration—begin by visualizing your mind as an actual room.

> Imagine that this room within your head has two holes in the front—open windows, you might say, like eyes to the world. And there are also two holes, where ears might be, on each side of the room.

Imagine that your tormentors are in this room, saying the things they have been saying in your internal dialogue. Watch them harassing, accusing, and infuriating you. When you are quite sure you've heard enough of their noise, you can take action.

Because you have extraordinary powers of imagination, you can change these intruders into squawking birds.

> The birds fly around the room that is your mind, making their rasping noises, flapping their wings frantically in the air, dropping feathers in their flurry.

When you are sure you have *really had enough,* order one of the birds to *fly out of your left ear!*

> Listen to the diminishing sound of its squawking, as it flies further away from your head.

Now demand that the other bird fly out of your right ear.

> Listen as it flies away and its sound diminishes in the distance.

Now that there are no more squawking birds in your head, take a huge vacuum cleaner and clean out all the feathers. Hose down the room, if necessary.

> Know that when you finish, your mind will be fresh and clear. The intrusive creatures cannot come back in because you won't give them permission.

From time to time you may hear the squawking from a distance. But just remember, the intruders can't return against your will.

Write this visualization down in your notebook; begin by naming the intruders and describing how they looked before and after you transformed them into birds.

Now take the pen in your non-dominant hand and name some other "birds" that keep making destructive noises in your head. You might consider devising your own exercise and see if you can discover another way to get them out of your thoughts.

Friendly intruders can also keep you from producing your best work. Sometimes they need to be dealt with before you can get on with your life. People you love need attention from you, but not necessarily during this work time. *If there is no one who has to have your attention at this particular time,* we can work on extracting your worries about them. If there's a chance that a baby will wake up and need your attention, or an elderly person will need care, then don't do the exercise; you want to remain receptive to their needs.

But if you know that for the rest of your work time there will not be any real demands for your attention, proceed with this exercise to help dispel your worrisome thoughts.

List a few of the people or situations that seem to draw your attention away from your work.

Now design a place in your mind that would provide perfectly for their needs for a few hours. If you are worried about a relative who is ill, imagine that person in a place where the finest doctors and nurses will take care of that person until you finish your work.

Imagine how comfortable and reassured that person will be by the highly competent and compassionate staff.

If you are worried about a teen-ager, then send that person to a special center where the boy or girl can have a long talk with one of the world's great therapists or advisors. Imagine that the person you love is suddenly quite receptive to the idea.

If you're worried about money, turn the situation over to the financial consultant who has found the solution to more monetary crises than anyone else in the country. Know that your affairs are in good hands for the next few hours.

Consider the list that you just made and the solutions you have designed. Know that the people *want* to go to those places (which, in some cases, is no small miracle in itself). You can even imagine how much they are going to thank you for designing that fantastic environment for them when they return after *your* work is finished.

Now send them on their way so you can get to work.

Take your pen in your other (non-dominant) hand and describe how it feels to be out from under your responsibilities for this short vacation from worry.

CATEGORY 6.
SENSORY STIMULATION

A Different Way of Feeling

Close your eyes and take a deep relaxing breath. Move the hand you usually write with across the back of your other hand and feel the bones and veins and skin texture, as you did on the first day of the program. Move your hand to touch some clothing on your body and be aware of the fabric, the texture, and temperature. Find another type of fabric on the chair or the floor and experience the difference.

> Open your eyes and touch
> something made of wood . . .
> something made of stone or glass.

Move around the room and find other tactile areas. Think of the differences, not with words, but with non-verbal, right-brain awareness of the uniqueness of each of these surfaces.

> If there is something in the room that has a great deal of intricate detail, run your hands along the surface and draw the detail with your fingers.

Now sit quietly for a moment with your eyes closed.

> Imagine that your hand is in warm water. Suddenly the water begins to cool and grow cooler and cooler still. Keep your hand in the water, even when it feels even cooler still. When the water becomes cold, *consider* removing your hand but let it stay just a moment longer. When the water has really become uncomfortably cold, remove your hand.

Now put your hand inside an imaginary soft blanket. Let the blanket become warmer, and warmer still. Let it be an electric blanket;

use your other hand to turn up the controls to HOT. Keep your hand inside the blanket until the warmth is uncomfortable, then pull it away.

If you have felt the changes in the temperature, even to a small degree, you have demonstrated again how much power your mind has over your body. (This exercise can be expanded to use on particularly cold or hot days.)

You have the potential, through mental imagery, to create the temperature you want in the room around you. Remember the yogis who can walk in freezing weather wearing only a light shirt? That kind of control would, of course, require years of study; most of us would feel satisfied if we could adjust our perception of temperature by five or ten degrees.

You can also play with your imagination and perception of tactile objects by using this exercise for recovering forgotten information.

> If there is something you would like to remember, use your senses to take you back to that time. Remember the *feel* of clothing, of heavy winter coats or scarfs, or sheer fabrics, or the feel of skin, or the smoothness of velvet.

Let your memory of touch carry you back a year, another and another . . . Rediscover something you have forgotten by remembering the sensation of touch.

CATEGORY 7.
FANTASY

You Are the Writer:
This Is Your Script

Imagine that you are a successful writer and you are sitting down to write a story. Be sure that you don't consult your left brain for the setting, the characters, or the plot. Your right brain has a story to tell, and if you will sit quietly and be receptive, the story will emerge.

Some writers begin with characters, others with plot, others with a visual picture.

Suppose you would like to begin by choosing a setting. Sit quietly while your mind wanders over the possibilities; be receptive to the images that emerge. (If you don't see a specific place in your mind, you can do yesterday's flying fantasy as a quick way to scan the earth and find your location.) When you have your first location, write about the place you have chosen: What do you see, hear, taste, feel, smell?

Sit quietly in the place that your right brain has chosen and wait for a character to approach you. It may be someone you didn't expect. What is the person like? What does that person feel? What is the specific dialogue that will begin your story?

Sit on the edge of the scene; watch and listen and feel and record what happens before your eyes. Sometimes you may want to "become" one of the characters and feel what happens from a particular point of view.

At another time, you may want to become one of the other characters and experience everything that is happening from that person's perspective. However you would like to do this is the proper way for you to proceed. Find your own way into the story in whatever way your right brain suggests to you now.

Begin to write your story. In it you can meet some interesting people. If the people and the story and the setting intrigue you enough, you can complete this script. Let the story unfold as you write.

If you want to know more about stories and how they are created, continue on to the next exercise.

CATEGORY 8.
DREAM WORK

Say Hello to the Producer
of Your Dream

You will recall Steve Allen's and Dr. James Grotstein's stories about a dream theater. Now you can draw from their enlightenment for your own dream work. In your notebook record a dream from last night or a previous night.

Take a deep relaxing breath. Close your eyes and imagine a room in which your dreams are created. This room, located in the right hemisphere of your brain, doesn't have to resemble a brain at all, for this is a fantasy. Imagine that room the way you would like it to be. You might find it helpful to see it as a darkened space where night creatures lounge about in its shadowy corners and where the dream's special producer sits in a place of comfort. There may be a tone of mystery in the room; it is, after all, the place of metaphors and dream symbols.

Walk slowly into the room. Let your eyes become accustomed to the dim light. Now that you are in the room, proceed slowly to the area of the producer and speak in a friendly way. Offer a gift to this creative personality. Perhaps you have brought cookies, or a bottle of wine, or flowers for the occasion. Explain to the producer that you have no wish to be intrusive, only to better understand the productions that are staged in your head each night. Explain that you often see fascinating pictures that confuse and bewilder you—sometimes (as good theater is wont to do) they even terrify you. (Praise is never a bad way to start any request, so I suggest you begin by thanking the producer for any entertaining or satisfying nighttime productions you can remember.)

Now ask your producer, who is surely one of the most creative parts of yourself, to please answer some questions you have regarding past performances. Why does a certain dream come back in replays like summer television shows? What message is there for you that you still have not comprehended? As much as you love mysteries, you love solutions even more. Ask the producer to explain what in last night's dream was unclear to you.

If your producer-self refuses to answer a question, trust the discretion of the inner self. Dream producers, who exist totally in the unconscious, know that sometimes the conscious mind is not ready to deal with the information hinted at in nighttime symbolism. Perhaps it is too soon for you to know the answers in full. Ask the producer what you can do to prepare for this information. If you still get no answer, ask for a clarifying dream that will lead you one step at a time toward understanding.

I suggest you do this with a light touch. It is never wise to push your producer around. Keep a respectful awareness of the creative gifts. Hold your dreams as you would a bird that rests most quietly in your open hand.

CATEGORY 9.
FREE ASSOCIATION

Morning Wisdom # 4

Set your timer for ten minutes, then write whatever comes to mind (and remember not to read it back until the sixth day). Remember, this exercise will put you in touch with unconscious material that can have very specific uses in your personal and professional life.

CATEGORY 10.
GIFTS FROM THE RIGHT BRAIN

Awareness Summary # 4

Find the most appropriate number on the Awareness Chart (on p. 129) and note it in writing.

Are you beginning to "feel the shift" as you move from one hemisphere to another? This comes easily to some people, while others find it very difficult. Be comfortable with either situation; your work is progressing and will continue to progress from now on. How fast you travel is not the issue; only the direction of your travel is important now.

Are you finding it easier to visualize? You might consider how real the cave and the cave paintings seemed to you in contrast to the house in the meadow on the first day. What changes do you notice in your visualization? What you see? Or taste? Or feel? Or smell? Or hear? Perhaps your greatest change may be in your ability to "go into" the experience. Describe the way it seems to you in your notebook.

In the script-writing exercise, did the characters resemble people you know? People you could see as extensions of yourself? Do you want to work with the characters again?

Make a list of the right-brain insights that came to you. (Also be aware of some ideas which still seem too elusive for words but which are struggling to be revealed.)

Remember how important it is to test right-brain desires against the analytic judgement of your left hemisphere before taking action.

CATEGORY 11.
AFFIRMATIONS

The Power Belongs to You

You have the power to use memories of the past to enrich the present, to use the happy times to nurture you, and to use the hard times as a catalyst for growth.

Program your left brain to accept the responsibility for your mood, your productivity, your success.

Copy the sentences of the following affirmations in your notebook and say them aloud:

I,_____, take the responsibility for the constructive use of my creativity.

Write the full sentence in your notebook.

Then imagine that someone very close to you is acknowledging that only you have the power over this decision:

You,_____, take the responsibility for the constructive use of your creativity.

Write the sentence in your notebook and say the words aloud, allowing the full meaning to imprint upon your mind.

Now imagine that someone who is very famous and highly respected is making this statement about you:

(Adjust the pronouns, if necessary!)

She,_____, takes the responsibility for the constructive use of her creativity.

Now program your right brain, your feeling self, with the following image:

With eyes closed, take a deep breath and find yourself in that special place you have imagined that is clearly accessible through your mind's eye. Imagine yourself sitting there quietly, attuned to the inner stillness that comes with this experience.

Imagine that several feet away from you there is an area that contains all the tools you need for the work you desire most to do. That area may contain a desk or table with the accouterments of your profession or your craft. Everything is there within that area—except your very self. You are seated at a distance, and around you are many good things that could distract you from the work you want to do. Fill in your own list of distractions: there might be a stereo or television, some golf clubs or a pile of "busy work." You have your own things in mind, so list them in your notebook.

Now visualize yourself walking past those distractions to the area where your work is to be done. Create a container for that area, such as a tent or some other enclosure around it. Seat yourself in the midst of this contained area.

Remain in that area for a few moments and allow yourself to feel the impact of the things around you. You may feel a subtle tingling along your spine that indicates your anticipation of the work you long to do.

Without words now, experience the feeling of responsibility that creative work entails. Feel the joy of it. Accept the fact that hard work is inherent in that joy. Hear the sounds of the world calling to you from outside the area of this containment, Then, with full cognizance of what you really want for yourself: Make your choice.

16

The Fifth Day

The place of silence within you is always available to you, no matter what anxieties the outer world may provide. You have the power to retreat to that place of relaxation and renewal whenever you choose.

Once you realize how much power you have over the extent of your body's relaxation, you will begin to comprehend the vast applications of right-brain techniques. Through the powers of your mind, you can create your own interior environment. You can use deep relaxation as a centering place from which to move toward high energy and creativity. And to a far greater extent than you may have realized, you have the power to allow success to be incorporated into your life.

Let your mind claim success, so that in your ordinary reality, you will be open to receive all the good things that will come to you.

As you settle into the comfortable chair in your work room, pay attention to what you are feeling and thinking. Consider your body tension and the energy level as you determine the number from the Awareness Chart (on p. 129) that most clearly defines what you are feeling now.

Focus on the words "deep relaxation" on the chart. As you look at the words, allow the deepest meaning possible to become a reality in your experience.

CATEGORY 1.
OUTSMARTING THE LEFT BRAIN

Mandala # 5

As you experience the mandala on the next page, try to spend a little more time with it than you have on previous days. Remember that you are trying to quiet the chatter of your inner voice as your right hemisphere deals with the spatial relationships of the pattern.

CATEGORY 2.
BIOFEEDBACK TRAINING

A Deeper Suggestion

Take a deep breath, breathing in through your nose. Hold the breath and gradually release it through your mouth. By now you are probably able to reach a state of deep relaxation just by taking this single deep breath. Let this biofeedback exercise take you even more into a state of deep relaxation.

> Be aware of the weight of your eyelids as they grow heavier and heavier until you want to close your eyes and feel the deep relaxation.

Let your concentration be on your feet

> as you tighten the muscles
> and hold . . . and relax.

Your feet feel warm and very heavy
and very relaxed.

> Concentrate on your legs

> > as you tighten and hold and relax.
> > Your legs feel warm
> > and heavy
> > and even more relaxed.

And now your buttocks

> tighten . . . hold . . . relax.

Your buttocks feel warm
and heavy
and relaxed.

And now your stomach . . .

tighten . . . hold . . . relax.
Your stomach feels warm
and heavy
and relaxed.

Now your hands . . .

tighten . . . hold . . . relax.
Your hands feel warm
and heavy
and relaxed.

And your neck . . .

tighten . . . hold . . . relax.
Your neck feels warm
and heavy
and relaxed.

Count down slowly from ten to zero.

10 . . .
As you count backwards,
feel your whole body relaxing
deeper and deeper
into a state of relaxation,
deeper and deeper . . .
9

Imagine you are walking down a long flight of stairs . . .

8
your relaxation is deeper and deeper
7
and you step down . . .
6
and down again
5
and feel more deeply relaxed

4
twice as relaxed
3
heavier
2
heavier and warmer
1
You feel wonderfully relaxed
completely at peace
deeper and deeper into relaxation.

When you are perfectly relaxed, imagine yourself stretched on a soft, inviting surface in that most wonderful retreat where you love to be, where you feel more creative than in any other place, where you find answers to problems quickly, where you release your intuitive powers and find the solutions that are best for you.

You may want to stay in this imaginary place a little longer—

Or you may want to count slowly from one to three and open your eyes feeling refreshed and alert.

Note the number on the Awareness Chart (on p. 129) that defines what you are feeling now.

CATEGORY 3.
GUIDED VISUALIZATION

Behind Closed Doors

Take the deep relaxing breath that tells your body you are ready to enter a state of right-brain awareness.

Imagine that you are walking down a long corridor with narrow walls and soft lighting. You can hear the sound of music in the distance, music that is vaguely familiar—as if you remember it from many years ago.

You reach the end of the corridor and there is a large, round room; around the room are doors and each door has a number.

Walk around the room and touch the handle of each door. The number on each door represents that year of your life, and each succeeding door opens onto a year further in the past. And of course you know that the choice will be yours and that you will be able to enter any door that you want to enter and experience whatever you want to experience from that year.

> There may be a door you should not enter; and if that is true for you, you will not enter through that door.

Choose a door that leads to a year that is significant for you and know that it is all right to choose a happy time or to choose a difficult time, but it is not all right to choose a time of devastating trauma, if such a thing ever happened to you in your life.

> Feel the handle of the door that you are most drawn to and observe the number; be most carefully aware of the number and then turn the handle and enter the room you have chosen.

When you step through that door, be aware that your body feels as it did in that year.

> And you are aware of the smells
> and the sounds
> and the feeling of that place.

You may be surprised at who you find there . . .

> Or maybe not. Maybe you knew all
> the time who would be waiting
> for you there.

Describe in your notebook what you see in that place.

Describe whom you see . . .

And what is said . . .

And what you needed to say then and what to say now . . .

And what you needed to hear then and want to hear now.

You may stay in this place a while longer if you want to. Or you may now count from one to three and return to the present and this place and the reality of your everyday life.

Perhaps the child who is still part of you, and who co-exists with the adult self that is also a part of you, discovered some new insight about that childhood time or reworked painful or disquieting feelings from that time. If that is the case, then record it in your notebook.

CATEGORY 4.
TRANSITIONAL OBJECTS

Turning Failure to Success

Almost everyone can remember an unpleasant event in childhood that has survived in the memory over the years. Some people try to repress those thoughts but sometimes find themselves drawn to the memory. Others have found it helpful to go into the feelings and "correct" the emotional conditioning. The reality of what happened is not as critical as our *response* to that reality. Fiction writers rework their pasts all the time. So can you.

> After you take the slow breath that signals deep relaxation, let your thoughts play backwards until you find the event you would like to work with.

Until you are experienced in reworking memories, it is best not to choose an event that is exceedingly traumatic. But you might choose a memory that involves something you did or said that caused people to reject you in some way. It is probably a memory that comes back to you often. Many people have an easily triggered memory that is associated with feelings of inadequacy. Decide now that you will re-work the memory to your advantage.

Decide that the memory will not be harmful to you in any way but will, in fact, create a healing association that will help you diffuse its power.

> Go into the feeling first by visualizing the place where this unpleasant event happened. You might want to recall the colors, the textures, the smells, even the taste that you experienced there. Now create the scene in your mind, including the feelings that seemed so overwhelming.

Stop the action of the scene at its most uncomfortable moment and imagine what you wish had happened. Create the action to make that happen. Remember: In fantasy, you have the power to make this happen. Diffuse the force of the event with this new action, this *re-creation*, that erases the negative associations and leaves you feeling good about yourself.

> Let the most rejecting person come forward and say something affirmative to you. Listen carefully as that person from your past says the words that make you feel good about yourself.

If there is someone there you wish would hug you and hold you and tell you that you are loved, let that person come forward and affirm you.

> If you have harbored hostility toward that person, prepare to release it now. If you find that hard even to consider, be aware of how destructive those hateful feelings have been as they dwelt inside you. Know that you can release the hatred, if you choose. If you don't want to forgive that person, then just act *as if you did* for just this one moment. Feel as if you have forgiven this person and realize what a calm and healing experience it is to forgive. Now consider your options again: Do you feel better forgiving the person or would you prefer to go back to the hateful feelings? The choice is yours.

CATEGORY 5.
OTHER-HAND WRITING

As If

Imagine something you would like to change about your life. It will be most useful to choose something you have wanted to change for a long time: negative patterns at home or at work, overeating, smoking, procrastinating. Choose your own situation.

Now imagine what it would be like if that change happened. Allow the feeling of that experience to be vivid in your imagination and visualize yourself as if success were already a reality. Take as long as you need to "see" yourself functioning in that different way. Write down what it would feel like if that became a reality. Make a list in your notebook of all the good things that would happen as a result of that change.

Now think of one thing you could do today that would begin to effect that change.

Now put the pen *in your non-dominant hand* and write a list of the things that would not be good about making that change. What would you have to give up? What price would you really have to pay if you made that change?

And, with either hand, write the answer to this question: *Do you really want to make that change?*

CATEGORY 6.
SENSORY STIMULATION

A Different Way
of Tasting/Smelling

Take a deep breath as you prepare to continue your explorations into the past. Close your eyes for a moment and let your thoughts drift away: Thoughts and words roll away from you, leaving a sense of stillness.

In your work room, at this moment:
Is the air fresh?
Are there flowers or potpourri close by?
Is the air stale from cigarettes or food? Put the back of your hand to your nose and be aware of any scent that lingers there . . . perfume or soap or lotion or . . .

Notice the taste that is in your mouth.

By concentrating on the smells or the taste associated with certain memories you can recall conversations and thoughts and feelings from that specific time.

Let your mind play backwards and recall some special moment worth remembering. Perhaps it was a month ago, or a year ago, or even longer than that. As I mention certain words, you will have an association to those words. Some of them may trigger very specific memories. Other words will not trigger associations, so allow them to pass freely through your mind without disrupting your concentration. See if any of these words suggest the memory of a certain smell or taste, and see where the recollection of those impressions takes you.

A certain scent may remind you of a certain person. You may choose to stop there and go into that memory. Or you may choose to let it go and move on to another association.

Smell the smoke of the fireplace or of cigarettes or of a brush-fire. . . . Let the following words scan slowly before your mind, suggesting images:

	pine needles
ocean	
	gymnasium
mothballs	
	pipe tobacco
freshly baked bread	
	hot berry pie
wine	
	lipstick
hair	
	attic
home	

If none of these words triggered an important memory for you, let your mind freely associate to other recollections and see where these connections take you.

Your senses are closely related to your experiences in the past. In the present, try to develop an appreciation of the five senses in your daily life. Soon you will start to notice many subleties you were unaware of before; *these subtleties may have nothing to do with specific senses but they will be stimulated by the senses.*

Through the development of this awareness, you will also begin to experience a heightened appreciation of the world about you.

Results From This
Right-Brain Experience

You have seen how sensory stimulation can revive memories and evoke intense emotions. And this can provide more than just an interesting experiment—as I discovered a few years ago.

My house was destroyed by a fire in the fall when Santa Ana winds (also known as "Santanas") start to blow across Southern California. The sight of heavy trees bending under hot, racing winds, the smell of dust and distant smoke, the sound of branches flailing themselves upon the house brought back every year thereafter intense feelings of anxiety. That was the case until one day I chose to write about those feelings, to allow them to surface with all of their power intact. Writing about the feelings had a "distancing" effect on them, and the result was that I no longer have the same intensity of fear when Santa Anas work their way across California every fall.

SANTANAS

Every year, in the California hills, *Santanas* blow;
'devil winds', the Indians called them long ago.
Air crackles from the heat; fires explode. Flames bite at parched and
    brittle grass, suck life from eucalyptus, birch and oak.
Every year,
choppers swoop and flail their wings like angry birds gone mad—
while sirens cry, wailing up twisted roads. Every year the hills burn.
    Malibu. Topanga. Beverly Glen. All have a turn.
In Bel Air, in '61, four hundred and fifty
houses burned.

Three times in as many years I packed from warnings—and all false.
Fourth time there wasn't time for anything
but running with babies and a dog
and a string of prayers across the hills.
Black sky turned mauve above the flames that rose to lick at stars.
I stayed away all night. Dawn came soon enough:
a fusion of melted things—silver, photographs and clothes,
woven with plaster and wood—draped like a quilt on an open grave.
Nothing stood. Nothing but chimneys,
stone markers where houses died.
Everything there, eaten alive.

I didn't build again. Some did.

But every fall, when *Santanas* start to blow,
I wake at night to the smell of fear and sense of loss.
Time turns 'round for awhile. Won't go on.
No matter how I try, the past holds strong.
What a strange thing, the human mind. Not to believe after all this
  time the danger's gone.

CATEGORY 7.
FANTASY

A Distant Place, A Backward Time

The power to recall any event of your past lies within your will.
Take a deep breath. Imagine that there is a large screen before you
and a projector by your side. In the palm of your hand are the controls
that allow you to flash any picture from your life onto the large screen.
People you knew and loved, people you never loved but wanted to love,
faces you only vaguely remember come onto the screen as you call
them forth. Your own picture may also appear on the screen.

> If you don't like a particular
> scene, you can press a button on the controls
> and it will disappear.

You may want to go back a few years,

> and a few more years.

You may want to go back even further,

> perhaps many years ago.

The choice is yours; you can see yourself at any age.

> Notice that someone special has come into the picture with
> you. Keep the picture in focus and remember how important
> that person was to you at the time.

Because of your extraordinary powers of imagination, you have
the ability to walk right into that picture and be that younger version
of yourself. The people there will seem real to you and your presence
in that distant time and place will seem real to you; you now have the
chance to say what you always wanted to say or what it occurs to you
now to say.

You have the ability to make the scene end if you want it to, and you will find yourself back in your chair in this present time and place. You also have the ability to continue the scene and rework any part of that happening that needs to be reworked.

You can make the scene end any way you want it to end.

And you can write any of your observations about what happened and the changes you made in the scene in your notebook.

CATEGORY 8.
DREAM WORK

Dialogue With the Actors

If your producer was helpful yesterday, you may want to return to visit him today with questions regarding last night's dream. If, on the other hand, you felt intimidated in the presence of such creative genius, perhaps you were unable to get the most out of your meeting. If that was the case, try talking to the actors themselves. First, choose one of your dreams (or dream fragments) from last night. Copy it in your notebook, along with your associations to the dream.

As you re-wrote the dream, did some other thoughts come to your mind?

Who is the principal character of the dream? Well, it was you, of course; you probably know that in dreams you often project your feelings onto another person. For example, it might seem that the subject of your dream was your child, your beloved, your best friend or worst enemy. In fact, your longings and fears are represented by each of these dream characters. You can see this for yourself, as you talk with each of the "actors" who act out the various parts of yourself.

Take a deep breath and, with eyes closed, allow yourself to enter the twilight territory where your dream was produced.

Meet with your dream producer and decide, intuitively, whether you want to discuss this matter with him or whether you should go directly to the actors themselves.

The actors are gathered at the set. The setting your producer-self chose in the dream is very important. Notice the details of the set.

Then, offer a gift to the entire cast. (Flowers perhaps, or candy?) This is a tangible expression of your good will. List the names (or descriptions) of the characters you remember now.

Later, you may remember other characters. If so, add them to your notebook's list.

Go first to the character with whom you feel the greatest empathy. To this friendly character, set several questions: "How did you feel last night, as those things happened to you . . .?" What was the character's reaction?

Then you can say to the actor, "I understand how you felt . . . I accept your feelings as valid, not at all_____ (create your own word: cowardly, ridiculous, foolish . . .)"
And then ask, "Is there anything you would like to tell me that was not made clear by what you felt or did in the dream?"

Now cross the dream stage and speak to a different dream character, someone who wasn't friendly or who was actually frightening. You can approach that character now, knowing that it exists in the twilight state but cannot hurt you if you don't allow it to. Ask several questions of that dream character: Go into the feeling of the dream. "Why did you want to hurt me?" or "Why were you so angry with me?" or . . . (create your own question).

There may be "characters" that are not people but, rather, are "characters" from nature, such as fire, or flood, or monsters of indescribable form. Approach each of them and ask these questions:
"Help me to understand you. What do you represent in the dream? What do you want from me?"

"Is there something about you that seems very similar to a quality that exists in me? Are there secrets you would like to reveal?"

When you leave the stage, take something with you that is pleasing to you—a gift from the actors, the sub-set of yourself. It could be any good thing that is worth bringing home with you: an affirmation, a promise, a poem, an insight.

CATEGORY 9.
FREE ASSOCIATION

Morning Wisdom # 5

Begin your free association and let the thoughts carry you wherever they will into whatever feelings and whatever hopes or fears come to mind. Let your mind spring from one place to another with ease. Remember not to read what you are about to write; tomorrow you will be given the technique for working with all of your free association exercises over the past few days. Now close your eyes a moment, let your mind wander, and then let your thoughts catch on a single word. Let that word be the first word in the first sentence of your free association.

CATEGORY 10.
GIFTS FROM THE RIGHT BRAIN

Awareness Summary

Note down the number from the Awareness Chart (on p. 129) that most accurately reflects what you are feeling now.

Are you beginning to see that you can define your creative energy and actually control it?

In your notebook, list the new insights that came as a result of your work. On some days your insights will be more in the personal area of your emotional growth. At other times the awarenesses will be regarding decisions you are trying to make for your more public life. Be open to whatever comes to you and remember that your right brain will sometimes provide answers to deep seated problems and ignore questions relevant to current issues.

It is wise to respond to whatever gifts are presented to you. No matter what your logical, questioning, left brain thinks, the intuitive right brain will give you answers according to its own priorities.

Present your right-brain suggestions to your left-brain critic and record any conflicts between them.

If compromise is indicated, what would each hemisphere suggest?

CATEGORY 11.
AFFIRMATIONS

A Value of the Gift

Mature creativity requires that you believe in yourself. You must believe that your hidden abilities exist and are emerging; believe in your right to take time to develop your gifts; believe that your creativity has value not only for yourself but for others as well. This conviction will allow you to rise above obstacles that could otherwise prevent you from expressing your creative talents.

All of these things are true, whether your talents are expressed in concert halls or board rooms, whether you work with your hands or your wits. Belief in yourself is basic—and hard to come by in a world that is often slow to nurture a developing spirit.

This affirmation will help you reinforce all the positive insights that have come to you in the last few days. Write your name with confidence in the blank spaces. Speak the words of assurance aloud as you write the following three sentences in your notebook.

I,_____, believe in the value of my creativity.

You,_____, believe in the value of your creativity.

She (He),_____, believes in the value of her (his) creativity.

Do you believe that in all the world you are unique? There is not another quite like you. And no one can create the music to the song of your life, except you. Some people may choose to compose a dirge—but you can choose a symphony of celebration.

To program your right hemisphere with confidence in this truth, use your slow, deep-breathing technique to make you receptive to this visualization:

Imagine that you are alone in your special place sitting with eyes closed. You don't need words to affirm you. Instead, go into that quiet place at the center of your being where you are able to feel the presence of your inner advisor. This may be the Wise Person you met in the secret cave or it may be some other advisor, who knows you better than even you know yourself. Find that someone who believes in you and in your potential. Wait quietly until you are aware of the presence of this special person. When you can feel the presence, look into the eyes of that person and allow the full meaning of this affirmation to be communicated into the deepest part of your being. Words are not necessary for this assurance:

You are a person of value and the work of your creative spirit will produce something of consequence for you and for others.

17

The Sixth Day

Discovering your creative powers and *mastering* your creative powers are two actions that carry equal weight on the scale that will weigh your success.

Discovery and mastery ride like children on each end of productivity's see-saw. At certain times, the high spot will be held by creative discovery, for you will confront new aspects of your potential all of your life. At other times, mastery of creative powers will be in the high spot, for this involves the *use* of those discoveries for producing the creative act. These are the twins that will play back and forth forever, sharing the joy of your work, balancing talent with commitment.

At the end of the sixth day, you will have achieved considerable excellence in developing both of these aspects of your potential.

By now, you probably have little or no difficulty defining your creative energy level through the use of the Awareness Chart. You may want to use the chart from time to time in the future, or you may feel, after today, that you are so much in touch with your level of creative energy that you don't need it to help you.

In either case, be sure to record your feelings on this sixth day, as you find the number from the Awareness Chart (on p. 129) that best defines what you are feeling now.

CATEGORY 1.
OUTSMARTING THE LEFT BRAIN

Mandala # 6

Each day as you use the mandala, you will discover greater value from the procedure. Perhaps you can spend an even longer period of time today focusing on the center of the design, allowing your peripheral vision to play with the form and structure. Be comfortable with the apparent movement of the form as the pattern seems to move in and out, to merge and part again.

Be particularly indifferent to the thoughts that drift into your awareness and move on. Allow them to arrive and to depart without your attention. Never try to force them away; whatever comes into your awareness will move out of consciousness as you allow the mandala to do its work.

Someday you may want to design your own mandalas. Many people find that very satisfying; and the addition of color will be interesting for you to experiment with.

For today, just allow the mandala to take you gently into your innermost place of silence

CATEGORY 2.
BIOFEEDBACK TRAINING

Mental Massage

This exercise works well for people with strong powers of imagination—and especially for those who respond well to body massage.

You will have to lie on your stomach to do this exercise. A carpeted floor will do nicely . . . the sofa, even better.

Lie on your stomach and take three very deep, even breaths, using the technique you have learned on the previous days.

Let your eyes close and your body respond to the stillness you feel. Drift down to a place of peace and inner silence.

Imagine that there is a person with you who has wonderfully soothing powers, someone who has the power to help you reach a state of deep relaxation.

Imagine that this person is placing soft, healing hands a fraction of an inch above your head.

All of your worries respond to the warmth that radiates from those hands, and very soon all thoughts flutter and drift away.

And you feel calm
and relaxed.

The hands touch your head and move down to touch your neck and then your shoulders. Any tightness in your neck and shoulders begins to diminish.

And you feel calm
and relaxed, and then
even more relaxed.

The hands encircle your left upper arm and slowly move down toward your elbow. As the hands pass each area of your arm, the tension in them drains away.

And you feel calm
and relaxed.

The hands move past your wrist and open your hand, pressing gently on the palm where pressure points are soothed.

You feel the warmth
and the faintest pressure.

Each finger, one by one, feels relaxed as the hands soothe the muscles.

And you feel calmer
And more deeply relaxed.

The hands return to your shoulders. The thumbs press each side of the top vertebrae of your spine. The fingers spread across your back. And the hands move slowly down your spine, relaxing each vertebrae as slowly, gently, the hands move. Very slowly, the hands move.

And you feel calm
and deeply relaxed.

The hands never lose contact with your body; they continue moving to your left leg, slowly moving down your thigh, as every muscle relaxes to the touch.

And you feel calm
and deeply relaxed.

Past your knee . . . your calf . . . your ankle . . .

And you feel calm
and perfectly relaxed.

The hands press against your heel, the instep . . . the ball of your foot . . . , soothing each toe until

you feel perfectly calm
and relaxed.

The hands keep contact with your body and massage the right side of your body until you are ready to move on to the next exercise. Then begin counting: one . . . two . . . *three*. Open your eyes and enjoy the relaxed and pleasurable feeling. Evaluate your feelings on the Awareness Chart (on p. 129) before you proceed to the section on guided visualization.

CATEGORY 3.
GUIDED VISUALIZATION

Stairway to the Past

Return to a state of deep relaxation. Enjoy that feeling of peace and erase your mind of all conscious thought. Then create a mental image of an imaginary, distant land. Let the land seem vaguely familiar, as if you have been there in a dream.

There is a high mountain and you are standing at its peak; you can see the vast landscape expanding far beneath you.

You may be surprised to find that there is a pathway formed of stone that leads down to a lower level. It is safe for you to walk there, and as you do, you count each stone step as you descend, slowly and safely, this natural stairway made of rock.

10
Descend even further

9

to a lower level.

8

As you walk down and down the
steps and landings and

7

you want to stop at one of the landings

6

you notice how easy it would be to step off the stairs onto one
of the landings.

5

And you begin to see familiar items arranged on one of the
landings a few yards below you. These things you recognize
from long years ago.

4

And you want to explore this landing

3

and you realize you are in a long-ago land in a house you lived
in when you were a child.

2

And you move smoothly into that old, familiar space . . . the
person who waits for you there is the most wonderful person
you remember from your childhood, and that person knows/
knew/has always known so very much and will tell you the
answer to any question you want to ask.

Who is the person waiting for you there?

What is the question you have always wanted to ask?

What is the answer that is given to you?

Very slowly on the count of one . . . two . . . three . . . , return to
your present age and to this work room.

Does the answer to the child's question have a bearing on issues
you are dealing with now in your adult life? Remember that while a
present situation can be very different from a past one, the feeling you
experience in the two situations may be quite similar.

CATEGORY 4.
TRANSITIONAL OBJECTS

Backward Motions

Imagine that you are again at the top of that high mountain. Look around you and describe the scene. Create the most beautiful place you can imagine. See this place at any time or season you choose. You may want to sit quietly and watch the sun rise, or you might design a warm summer evening and enjoy the stars. Enjoy your power and freedom to choose your environment. If one season or vista is not exactly right for you, experiment and choose another. Write down what you see in your mind's eye.

A large telescope is not far away. It is an instrument of great power and fantastic abilities. Walk over to it and point it toward the distant past; let the telescope scan the following items until one of them hooks your attention:

airplane

car

boat

train

bicycle

tricycle

roller-
skates

ice skates

skateboard

skiis

sled

wagon

horse

(or any other means of
transportation that
pleases you.)

Let your mind attach to the transitional object until it carries you into a specific memory. Write in your notebook what you remember and how you feel.

Is there something this memory brought forth that is of value to you now? Is there anything about it that parallels some feelings you've been having lately? If something comes clearly to mind, write it down; if not, write out the first thoughts that come to mind about your present life.

Be aware of how your mind ties the past and the present together by long strings of memory over which you have great control. If some new awareness comes to your attention, write it down.

Through the powers of your mind, all of the past is available to you. When you want a deeper understanding of your feelings, visit the child that you were and learn to listen to the messages that child conveys to you. At any time, you can travel back to any age. You can retrieve any feeling or memory that is worth transporting into the present.

CATEGORY 5.
OTHER-HAND WRITING

Word Sketch

Think of a person who stirs a strong negative emotion in you. It could be a person you fear or dislike or disrespect. It could be a person you know very well or a person you know only through working with him or her in a specific situation. Write the person's name in your notebook.

Write a description of that person, beginning with physical attributes and then moving on to personality and character traits. Capture as much of the passion of your feelings about this person as you can in this word sketch.

Now take your pen in the non-dominant hand. How many of these attributes could also apply to you? Are there things you hate or fear or resent in that person that relate in any way to things you hate or fear or resent about yourself? Explore this idea by using your other hand to write your response to the question.

Now, shift back to your usual writing hand and see if you can remember any situation that caused you to show some of these same characteristics.

Are there any changes you would like to make in yourself because of this exercise?

Are there any changes you want to make in the way you relate to the person you described?

Can you find something about that person that might explain why he or she is causing you to have such strong feelings?

Can you think of something you may have done to provoke these feelings?

Are you a threat to that person?

Is that person a threat to you?

Think of the last couple of times you've had contact with that person. Did you do something to make the situation better or something that made it worse?

If the situation is tantalizing enough for you, you might want to create a visualization where you go back to the Caring Person in the cave (or to wherever you like to meet your inner advisor). Ask some questions about your feelings and how you can understand them more clearly and use them constructively.

CATEGORY 6.
SENSORY STIMULATION

A Different Way of Knowing

There are many ways we perceive information about people. Beyond the most obvious, everyday ways are more subtle ones: We "read" body language or the silences between the words; we watch the sudden changes around the eyes or the quick tightening of muscles in the throat.

Part of what is called the "sixth sense" is actually keen observations we make that slip unnoticed past the conscious mind but which are imprinted upon our unconscious awareness. Intuition is far more than this, of course. It's a process that functions outside of scientific understanding. Intuition is impossible to manipulate, but we can invite this "different way of knowing" into our consciousness when we are in a state of relaxed readiness. Paying attention to your hunches, messages, or any extrasensory experiences can increase your sensitivity in many critical areas.

I'm not suggesting you put all your trust in "magical thinking." I'm only suggesting that you use the innate right-brain powers that are part of your natural potential and be open to the information that your right brain is suggesting. There is no magic here, only the use of your gifts in a fuller capacity.

> Close your eyes and let that deep breath create a receptive state for visualization. Allow yourself to go as deeply into a twilight state as possible. You may want to count backwards, slowly, from ten to one. You may want to imagine walking down a flight of stairs or descending a long ramp. Feel as if you were enveloped in a sensation of warmth and heaviness. Create whatever situation is best for you until you reach that intense concentration that closes out all thoughts and you are ready to receive the messages your unconscious mind is willing to release to you.

In your mind's eye, create a dream stage. Invite the director of your dreams to join you and sit beside you as you watch the dream theater.

> You can create your own dream, and, with the help of a full cast and crew, you will be able to choose the theatrical production most beneficial for you now.

Design a set that is laced with fog and lit with dim, softly-colored lights. Let the fog create a mysterious curtain between you and the cast. Now let the stage be filled with people who are not clearly visible through the mist.

> Notice that one of the characters comes forth, moving through the fog into your line of vision; let that person remain before

you a moment and then move it back into the fog. And now another figure comes forward; others too, one at a time, in any way that the director calls them forth.

If any of the people have something to say to you, listen carefully. Allow the actors to improvise the script. Listen without comment and attend to the meaning behind those comments. It is possible that one of those people will want to be alone with you for a while, to come closer; if so, let it be. This is your dream theater and the cast is peopled with those who have been part of the drama of your life, both past and present (perhaps even from your future).

If there is something you need to say to any person in the cast, say it now. Be receptive to whatever insights come to you, whatever needs are expressed, whatever longings emerge. Be conscious of *any* new information.

When you are ready to come back to your workroom, count slowly from one to three and open your eyes.

It may be that your intuition spoke to you through the characters in the play. Or you may need to return to the theater again, at another time, if the actors spoke too softly for you to hear the messages they were trying to convey.

If this visualization led you to feel that someone needs help from you, attend to that feeling. In reality, it may or may not be valid, but it is worth checking out, just to be sure.

CATEGORY 7.
FANTASY

Journey to a Strange Planet

Imagine that you are living in the distant future, hundreds of years from this present age. Scientific knowledge has advanced at a compounded rate and technological possibilities are limitless. You are preparing to take a journey to a place where you have never been before. Time is not a factor; all of outer space is the new frontier. Do not be bound by the realities of your present understanding of science. Hundreds of years ago, scientists could not have fathomed the things we now accept as part of everyday life.

Your space ship is waiting and you have said goodbye for now to people you love. You plan to be back in a matter of a few weeks.

Imagine yourself ready to enter the space ship. As a last thought, you remember that there was something you wanted to take with you—and suddenly it appears before your eyes. There seems to be no reason to take this item with you, but you sense that it is something you want very much to have with you. Write the name or description of the item you plan to take.

Your space ship will be launched from a clearing among dense trees—you might envision a forest or even a jungle where the ship appears to have been hidden. Step inside the space ship, which has complete 360-degree visibility, and look into the surrounding trees, where you can see movement. There is an animal rushing toward you, wanting to come with you. Impulsively, you open the door and invite it in. Describe the animal you are taking and give it the first name that comes to your mind.

All you need to do now is press a button and the space ship takes off. Enjoy the sensation of lifting off above the earth. Enjoy the sense of speed and power and freedom. Imagine how it feels to look down on stars, to pass the moon, to know that your space ship is equipped to take you anywhere you want to go. Relax and enjoy the experience.

When you see the planet you want to visit, direct your space ship for landing. Be sure your landing is safe and easy. When you step out, you are in a place you have never been before. You open the door and look around. The animal that came with you stays close by your side. You reach for the item you brought from earth and step out of the space ship.

Describe in your notebook what you see and what you feel.

And then what happens?

What does the animal do?

Find a use for the item you brought with you (if you haven't done so already).

When you are ready to return to earth, get back in the space ship. Will the animal return with you? Will you take the item you brought from earth with you? How does it feel to leave?

You are traveling toward earth and you see it far in the distance. How do you feel about coming home?

When the space ship has landed safely, open the door and look around to see if anyone has come to meet you. How do you feel about seeing that person?

Create your own ending to the story, if anything seems unresolved. Then close your eyes and discover that you are already back in your work room. Slowly open your eyes and consider the events in your story. Who or what did the animal represent? What did it do for you (or you for it)? Why do you suppose you chose that particular animal? (A clue might come from considering the attributes generally associated with that kind of animal.) If you chose your own pet, you might be holding on to the familiar—a security blanket, of sorts. If you chose a friendly lion, was it there to protect you? If you chose a kitten, what do you suppose that means?

Remember what it was like on that strange and distant planet? How does it represent life as you would like it to be—or you are afraid it will be? Are there indicators in this story that show you some of your specific desires or fears? In your notebook, clarify any insights you brought back with you from the far-away planet.

CATEGORY 8.
DREAM WORK

Programming Your Messenger

Record a dream, or dream fragment, from last night.

Now write your associations to it, using the techniques you have learned in this program.

Re-create the dream in your mind's eye and focus on any images that seem to be calling for your attention. Begin to devise your own style for dream work: Do you want to be the characters? Or to call in your dream producer? Or try the Senoi techniques? Play with these ideas and choose one to explore in your notebook.

Tonight, try programming your dreams. Before you go to bed, decide what specific problem you would like your dream producer to work on. Make the request as direct as possible and, most of all, *be very sure that you want to know the answer.* Make the question as direct as: "Do I really want this job?" "Is there one thing I could do to make this problem easier?" "Do I really want to go through with my plans to . . .?"

After you go to bed, focus on this one question. Create a visualization in which you tell your dream producer that you need help. Ask that clues be given to you through dreams that will help you understand how your right brain feels about your situation.

Be sure to keep a paper and pen beside you in the night and be ready to write down the answer. (You may want to use a pen that has a tiny built-in flashlight at the writing end and avoid turning on bright lights.)

CATEGORY 9.
FREE ASSOCIATION

Interpreting Morning Wisdom

For the last six days, you have written during this category, and unless your curiosity got the best of you, you haven't read that material since you wrote it. Now it's time to learn how to use these free associations. The writer S. L. Stebel told me about this technique for discovering your personal metaphors. It works, not only for writers, but for anyone interested in discovering the coded messages of the unconscious.

Go back over each day's writing and circle the phrases that hold the greatest interest for you. Try to be sensitive to hidden meanings. When you finish each day's writing, read the circled metaphors again and ask yourself these questions:

- Is there an emotional pattern, a recurrent thread, that is woven through all (or some) of these?

- Is there a relationship between these circled phrases and other feelings that I have been thinking about—or tried to *avoid* thinking about?

- Has anything been revealed that gives me new insight into some particular problem?

After you have circled all the important phrases, metaphors, and surprises, write them in a list. This list will reveal the secrets your unconscious mind is willing to share. Deeper insights, which you are not yet prepared to receive, will be withheld for your own sake. A prudent dream producer should not allow certain things to be expressed until he or she is able to receive the information in an appropriate way.

CATEGORY 10.
GIFTS FROM THE RIGHT BRAIN

Awareness Summary

Note the number from the Awareness Chart (on p. 129) that describes how you are feeling now.

In the preceding days, you have explored many aspects of your feelings and touched upon memories and desires that have emerged from the darkness of your unconscious mind.

From all the insights that surfaced during the days you have used this program, you may have discovered a strong desire to express a particular talent or a certain aspect of your creativity.

In *The Eighth Day of Creation* Elizabeth O'Conner wrote, "If our unused gifts have any strength or power of their own, they cry out for recognition—to be given a name. They are not only disturbers of our sleep; they make our days uneasy." In your notebook, name the gift that calls to you from your dreams and your fantasies.

If you found it difficult to name that gift, consider what you would really love to do. Sometimes the intense desire to do a specific thing will call forth the angel, and you will discover greater talent in that area than you ever realized. Love what you do, and the doing of it will not only give you satisfaction but will continually produce finer work.

Make a list of the types of creative activities that give you the greatest pleasure.

Is there some activity you would like to develop but feel shy about pursuing (such as singing or skating or mountain climbing or anything else that you would love to do just for the sheer joy of it)? Describe in your notebook how good it would feel to do that activity, even if other people thought it was a silly thing to do.

In *Moments,* the artist/poet Corita wrote:
"Love the moment and the energy of that moment will spread beyond all boundaries."

Mature creativity demands commitment. To nurture your talent requires considerable discipline, for there are many other good things you will not have time to do if you are serious about your creativity. Allot a specific time each week for the development of your gifts. Write down the days you will work and the specific time each day.

Think back over the categories of exercises you have enjoyed during this program. List the ones that have provided the greatest benefit for you.

Decide the most effective way you can incorporate them into your work schedule: Will you continue to keep a dream journal? Will you use the biofeedback training on a daily basis to help sustain your creative energy? What specific plans do you have to use these and other right-brain techniques in the future?

Set goals for yourself, and in your notebook define those goals as clearly as you can.

CATEGORY 11.
AFFIRMATIONS

The Emerging Spirit

I have one last affirmation to share with you before you move on beyond this book to chart your own creative future.

Speak these words softly, with calm conviction, as you write your name in these sentences in your notebook.

I,_____, use my creativity for my pleasure, my fulfillment, and my success.

Then write your name again in the blank space, and listen to the words as if you were hearing them from someone you love who is very proud of you and who encourages you to fulfill your potential.

You,_____, use your creativity for your pleasure, your fulfillment and your success.

And finally, listen to these words of affirmation as if they were spoken by someone you have tried to please for a very long time:

She (He),_____, uses her (his) creativity for her (his) pleasure, fulfillment and success.

Now, create the place in your mind's eye that is special for you and sit quietly as you have on previous days. With your eyes closed, find the center of silence that is within you and respond to the feeling of peace and well-being that attends the silence.

In that place in your mind's eye, invite your inner advisor to join you. If it seems appropriate, offer a gift that will be pleasing to this Wise and Caring Person, who accepts you without qualifications and wishes only the best for you.

Let the hands of that person rest gently upon your head. Feel the love and the healing spirit transfer from that powerful being through sensitive fingertips into your very self. Be aware that this message is being communicated from that person of great wisdom to all parts of your body and mind.

Accept the full meaning of the affirmation that is communicated to you without words through a deeper awareness of truth.

May the words of this affirmation be true for you all the days of your life.

Notes

Testing procedures that enable researchers to understand how each hemisphere functions for specific activities include:

THE WADA TEST

> When either hemisphere is anesthetized, the functions of its partner become clearly observable. Doctors routinely use a procedure, called the Wada test, on brain-damaged patients prior to surgery to determine the dominant hemisphere. Sodium amytal is injected into the artery that leads to either the left or the right hemisphere of the brain. This anesthetizes half of the brain and allows doctors to observe how patients use the unaffected hemisphere. Later they can reverse the procedure and observe how the other hemisphere performs. The results of their tests confirm the validity of the split-brain findings with regard to hemisphere specializations.

There are also tests for people who have healthy brain functions, and these concur with the findings obtained from these clinical patients.

TACHISTOSCOPE

> Using the tachistoscope, the researcher controls which hemisphere first receives specific information. Then, by measuring the time it takes for the person to react, the researcher can determine which hemisphere is specialized for that particular task.

POSITRON TOMOGRAPHY

> The positron tomograph is an instrument that can photograph each half of the brain; it is activated by specific stimuli or specific activity. This device allows researchers to observe the healthy brain in action. It works by measuring hemispheric cerebral glucose utilization. Radioactive material, injected into the bloodstream, flows into the brain, allowing doctors to photograph metabolic activity in the hemispheres for as long as forty minutes after the injection is given.

ELECTROENCEPHALOGRAPH (EEG)

> Electrodes are placed over the temporal and parietal lobe on both sides of normal subjects' brains before they are given various tests. The EEG records the type of brain activity generated during these mental tasks. High-voltage, slow alpha

waves indicate a "relaxed" hemisphere; and low-voltage, fast beta waves indicate a "working" hemisphere.

DICHOTIC LISTENING TEST

In dichotic testing, two channels of conflicting information are presented to a person simultaneously, one channel to each ear. Input to the right ear is conveyed to the left hemisphere and vice versa. The subject will report hearing only the information which was received by the hemisphere specialized for that type of input (for example, language in the left hemisphere, music in the right).

If you would like to know more about the research in split brain studies and cerebral lateralization, I recommend the following sources in the bibliography:

For the general reader: Blakeslee, Ferguson, Jaynes, Ornstein, Sagan, Springer and Deutsch.

For readers with scientific interests: Bogen, Davidson, Dimond, Franco, Galin, Gazzaniga, Gordon, Gur, Hoppe, Levy, Nebes, Sackeim, Schwartz, Sperry, and Zaidel.

For information regarding tapes, seminars and other right-brain materials, please contact:

Right Brain Resources
Reseda Medical Building
7012 Reseda Boulevard Suite SW 101
Reseda, California 91335
Att: Eleanore Kubiak

Bibliography

Adams, James L. *Conceptual Blockbusting*. 2nd ed. New York: W.W. Norton, 1974.

Andersen, Marianne S. and Louis M. Savary, et al., eds. *Passages: A Guide for Pilgrims of the Mind*. New York: A Collins Associates Book, Harper and Row, 1972.

Arguelles, Jose and Mariam. *Mandala*. Boulder and London: Shambhala, 1972.

Arieti, Silvano. *Creativity: The Magic Synthesis*. New York: Basic Books, 1976.

Austin, James H. *Chase, Chance, and Creativity*. New York: Columbia University Press, 1978.

Blakeslee, Thomas R. *The Right Brain*. Garden City, New York: Anchor Press/Doubleday, 1980.

Bogen, J.E. "The Other Side of the Brain: II. An Appositional Mind." *Bulletin of the Los Angeles Neurological Societies* 34 (1969) pp. 135–162.

Bogen, J.E. and Bogen, B.M. "The Other Side of the Brain: III. The Corpus Callosum and Creativity." *Bulletin of the Los Angeles Neurological Societies* 34 (1969) pp. 191–217.

Bogen, J.E. and M.S. Gazzaniga. "Cerebral commissurotomy in man. Minor hemisphere dominance for certain visuospatial functions." *Journal of Neurosurgery* (1965) pp. 394–399.

Bogen, Joseph and David Macaulay. "A Walk through a Giant Brain." *Human Nature* (October 1978) pp. 40–47.

Bressler, Dr. David E. with Richard Trubo. *Free Yourself from Pain*. New York: Simon and Schuster, 1979.

Bruner, Jerome. *On Knowing*. Expanded edition. Cambridge: Harvard University Press, 1962.

Bry, Adelaide with Marjorie Bair. *Directing the Movies of Your Mind*. New York: Harper and Row, 1978.

Capacchinone, Lucia. *The Creative Journal*. Athens, Ohio: Swallow Press Books, 1979.

Caruso, Charles. "Creativity as Enigma." *MD* (April 1982) pp. 139–146.

Corita. *Moments*. Boston: Beacon Press. 1982.

Davidson, Richard J. and Gary E. Schwartz. "Brain Mechanisms Subserving Self-Generated Imagery: Electrophysiological Specificity and Patterning." *Psychophysiology* (1977).

Davis, Martha, Ph.D., et. al. *The Relaxation & Stress Workbook*. Richmond, CA: New Harbinger Publications, 1980.

Delaney, Gayle M.V., Ph.D. *Living Your Dreams*. San Francisco: Harper & Row, 1979.

Dimond, S.I., Farrington, L., and Johnson, P. "Differing Emotional Response from Right and Left Hemispheres." *Nature* 261 (1976) pp. 690–692.

Edwards, Betty. *Drawing on the Right Side of the Brain*. Los Angeles: J.P. Tarcher, Inc., 1979.

Epstein, G. *Waking Dream Therapy: Dream Process as Imagination*. New York: Human Sciences Press, 1981.

Ferguson, Marilyn. *The Brain Revolution*. New York: Bantam Books, 1975.

Franck, Frederick. *The Zen of Seeing*. New York: Random House, 1973.

Franco, L. and R.W. Sperry. "Hemisphere Lateralization for Cognitive Processing of Geometry." *Neuropsychologia* 15 (1977) pp. 15, 107–114.

Galin, David, M.D. "Implications for Psychiatry of Left and Right Cerebral Specialization." *Arch. Gen. Psychiatry* 31 (October 1974) pp. 572–583.

Garfield, Patricia L., Ph.D. *Creative Dreaming*. New York: Simon and Schuster, 1974.

Gawain, Shakti. *Creative Visualization*. Mill Valley, California: Whatever Publishing, 1978.

Gazzaniga, Michael S. *The Bisected Brain*. New York: Appleton-Century-Crofts, 1970.

Geschwind, Norman. "Specialization of the Human Brain." *Scientific American* 241, No. 3 (September 1979) pp. 180–199.

Ghiselin, Brewster. *The Creative Process: A Symposium*. New York: New American Library, 1952.

Gordon, H.W. "Hemispheric asymmetries in the perception of musical chords." *Cortex* (1971) pp. 387–398.

Gordon, H.W., and J.E. Bogen. "Hemispheric Lateralization of Singing after Intracorotid Sodium Amylobarbitone," *J. Neurol., Neuros., and Psychiat.* 37, No. 6, p. 727.

Grotstein, James S. ed. *Do I Dare Disturb the Universe? a Memorial to Wilfred R. Bion*. Beverly Hills: Caesura Press, 1981.

Hampden-Turner, Charles. *Maps of the Mind*. New York: Macmillan, 1981.

Hoppe, Klaus D., M.D. "Split Brain—Psychoanalytic Findings and Hypotheses." *Journal of the American Academy of Psychoanalysis* 6, No. 2 (1978) pp. 193–213.

Hoppe, Klaus D., M.D. "Split Brains and Psychoanalysis." *Psychoanalytic Quarterly* Vol. XLVI (1977) pp. 220–244.

Hoppe, Klaus D. and Joseph E. Bogen. "Alexithymia in Twelve Commissurotomized Patients." *Psychotherapy and Psychosomatics.* 28 (1977) pp. 148–155.

Jaynes, Julian. *The Origin of Consciousness in the Breakdown of the Bicameral Mind.* Boston: Houghton Mifflin Company, 1976.

Jung, Carl G. *Man and His Symbols.* Garden City: Doubleday & Company, 1964.

———. *Memories, Dreams, Reflections.* New York: Random House, 1961.

Kimura, D. "Left–Right Differences in the Perception of Melodies." *Quarterly Journal of Experimental Psychology* 16 (1964) pp. 355–358.

Koestler, Arthur. *The Act of Creation.* New York: Macmillan, 1964.

Levy, Jerre, Robert D. Nebes and Roger W. Sperry. "Expressive language in the surgically separated minor hemisphere." *Cortex* 7 (1971) pp. 49–58.

Levy, J., C. Travarthen, R.W. Sperry. "Perceptions of Bilateral Chimeric Figures following Hemispheric Deconnexion. *Brain* 95 (1972) pp. 61–78.

Lightman, Alan. "Science on the Right Side of the Brain." *Science 82,* pp. 28–29.

Masters, Robert and Jean Houston. *Mind Games.* New York: Dell, 1972.

May, Rollo. *The Courage to Create.* New York: W.W. Norton, 1975.

McKim, Robert H. *Experiences in Visual Thinking.* 2nd ed. Monterey, California: Brooks/Cole Publishing Company, 1972.

Nebes, R.D. "Superiority of the minor hemisphere in commissurotomized man for the perception of part–whole relations." *Cortex* (1971) pp. 333–349.

O'Conner, Elizabeth. *Eighth Day of Creation.* Waco, Texas: Word Books, 1971.

Olson, Robert W. *The Art of Creative Thinking.* New York: Barnes & Noble, 1978.

Ornstein, Robert E. *The Psychology of Consciousness.* New York: Penguin Books, 1975.

———. ed. *The Nature of Human Consciousness.* San Francisco: W. H. Freeman and Company, 1973.

———. "The Split and Whole Brain." *Human Nature* 1, No. 5 (May 1978) pp. 76–83.

Plimpton, George, ed. *Writers at Work; The Paris Review Interviews,* Fifth Series. New York: Penguin Books, 1981.

Proust, Marcel. *Swann's Way* (Trans. C.K. Scott Moncrieff). New York: Random House, 1928.

Rainer, Tristine. *The New Diary.* Los Angeles: J.P. Tarcher, Inc., 1978.

Rainwater, Janette, Ph.D. *You're in Charge.* Los Angeles: Guild of Tutors Press, 1979.

Restak, Richard M. "The Brain." *The Wilson Quarterly.* (Summer 1982) pp. 89–113.

Sackeim, Harold A. and Ruben C. Gur. "Lateral Asymmetry in Intensity of Emotional Expression." *Neuropychologia,* 16, pp. 473–481.

Sagan, Carl. *The Dragons of Eden.* New York: Random House, 1977.

Samples, Bob. *The Metaphoric Mind: a Celebration of Creative Consciousness.* Reading, Mass.: Addison-Wesley, 1976.

Samuels, Mike, M.D., and Nancy Samuels. *Seeing with the Mind's Eye: The History, Techniques and Uses of Visualization.* New York: Random House, 1975.

Schulz, Charles M. *Classroom Peanuts.* New York: Holt, Rinehart and Winston, 1982.

_____. *Thank Goodness for People.* New York: Holt, Rinehart and Winston, 1976.

Schwartz, G.E. and R.J. Davidson and F. Maer. "Right Hemisphere Lateralization for Emotion in the Human Brain: Interactions with Cognition." *Science* 190 (1975) pp. 286–288.

Simonton, Carl O., Stephanie Matthews-Simonton, and James L. Creighton. *Getting Well Again.* New York: Bantam Books, 1980.

Sperry, Roger. "Some Effects of Disconnecting the Cerebral Hemispheres." Nobel Prize lecture, 8 December 1981.

Sperry, R.W., E. Zaidel, and D. Zaidel. "Self Recognition and Social Awareness in the Disconnected Minor Hemisphere." *Neuropsychologia* 17, pp. 153–166.

Springer, Sally P. and Georg Deutsch. *Left Brain, Right Brain.* San Francisco: W.H. Freeman and Company, 1981.

Teresi, Dick ed. "Behavior and the Mind." *Omni's Continuum: Dramatic Phenomena from the New Frontiers of Science.* Boston: Little, Brown and Company, 1982. pp. 91–122.

Tucker, D.M. "Lateral Brain Function, Emotion, and Conceptualization." *Psychological Bulletin* 89 (1981) pp. 19–46.

Winnicott, D. "Transitional Objects and Transitional Phenomena." *Int. Journal of Psychoanalysis,* 34 (1953) p. 89.

Young, John G., M.D. "Toward a Definition of Creativity." *MD* (January 1982) pp. 27–29.

Zaidel, E. "Auditory Language Comprehension in the Right Hemisphere Following Cerebral Commissurotomy and Hemispherectomy: A comparison with Child Language and Aphasia." *Language Acquisition and Language Breakdown*, ed. A. Caramazza and E. Zurif. Baltimore: Johns Hopkins, 1978.

Zaidel, E., D.W. Zaidel and R.W. Sperry. "Left and Right Intelligence: Case Studies of Raven's Progressive Matrices following Brain Bisection and Hemidecortication." 1981.

Index

About the Author

Marilee Zdenek has led seminars on the subject of creativity since 1970. For the last four years, she has been on staff at the Santa Barbara Writers Conference, where many of the concepts of this book were first tested. She is president of *Right-Brain Resources, Inc.*, a California-based company specializing in programs and materials related to the creative experience. During the last fifteen years, she has served on the Board of Directors of three hospitals and a surgical/diagnostic eyecare facility. *The Right-Brain Experience* is Ms. Zdenek's fifth book. She is also the author of *Splinters in My Pride* and *Someone Special*. *God Is a Verb!* and *Catch the New Wind* were written in collaboration with Marge Champion. Ms. Zdenek lives in Los Angeles with her husband, Albert N. Zdenek, M.D., and has two grown daughters.

Catalog

If you are interested in a list of fine Paperback
books, covering a wide range of subjects
and interests, send your name and address,
requesting your free catalog, to:

McGraw-Hill Paperbacks
1221 Avenue of Americas
New York, N.Y. 10020